HOUSTON 2020

HOUSTON 2020

America's Boom Town - An Extreme Close Up

RALPH BIVINS

COPYRIGHT

Copyright © 2018 Ralph Bivins through Fifth Estate Media LLC

All rights reserved.

No part of this book may be reproduced in any form or by any electronic or mechanical means, including information storage and retrieval systems, without written permission from the author, except for the use of brief quotations in a book review.

Published by Fifth Estate Media, Winter Garden, Florida

Printed in the United States of America

Author photograph by John Everett

Cover illustration by Jesse Kunerth

Editing by Mary Shanklin

Copy editing by Laureen Crowley

U.S. Library of Congress cataloging publication

Houston 2020: America's Boom Town – An Extreme Close Up

DEDICATION

This book is dedicated with gratitude to my dear family for their support, encouragement and endurance. And thank you to my parents who sacrificed to care for me without failing.

I am indebted to the thousands of real estate professionals who took the time – on many occasions over the years – to explain the trends and projects that became real estate news, my specialty as a journalist.

The list of these helpful people from Houston and around the country includes home builders, brokers, developers, investors, architects, economists, hoteliers, retailers, mortgage bankers, elected officials, planners, attorneys and many others.

CONTENTS

Introduction	ix
Foreword	xi
Preface	xiii
1. The Soul of Houston	1
2. Three Wise Men: Lessons Learned	15
3. The Resilient City	24
4. Downtown Skyscrapers and Their Struggle to Remain Relevant	42
5. The Grand Parkway: America's Longest Loop	56
6. Highrise Surge: Houstonians Without Yards – or Cars	71
7. The Marketing Genius of the Energy Corridor	83
8. Adaptive Reuse and Houston's 72 Million Square-Foot Bubble	96
9. Parks: The Catalytic Converter	107
10. A New Landmark: The Texas Medical Center's Double Helix	120
11. The Galleria: Let There Be Light	130
12. Pierce Elevated: Tear Down This Wall	142
13. E-Commerce, Plastics and the Unseen Engine	150
About the Author	161

INTRODUCTION

By Dr. JAMES P. GAINES, Chief Economist Real Estate Center at Texas A&M University

The history of Texas can easily be defined as a grand real estate campaign. Texas real estate development traces from the earliest settlements establishing a series of missions by the Spanish to Stephen F. Austin's energetic promotion of the state by providing land grants to the early settlers who created vast ranches, such as the huge King Ranch in south Texas. Development also sprang from the early land promotion schemes of the Allen brothers, who founded the City of Houston. In short, the history of the state can readily be described in terms of land promotions, land development schemes and a rush to acquire a piece of Texas.

In the early 20th Century, land promotion was fueled by the state's famous Spindletop oil discovery in 1901 and the subsequent rush for oil. As the Texas population swelled and land development became even more intense, major metropolitan centers emerged that today rank among the largest, most prosperous and most dynamic in the country – Dallas and Houston. Dallas became the southwestern financial and distribution hub thanks to the combination of the rail lines and highway systems, and Houston became the global energy capital of world

INTRODUCTION

as the center of the oil and gas exploration and production and the petrochemical industry.

By the later part of the century, Texas, and Houston in particular, achieved status as a center for innovative and creative real estate development activity as well as the home of major players, not only in the state, but throughout the country and the world. Trammell Crow, Gerald Hines, George Mitchell and others emerged as pioneers in real estate development and brought with them innovative and creative concepts of design, processes, architecture and new, innovative images of the urban landscape, not only for Texas cities but elsewhere as well. Houston became not only the energy capital of the world, but also the home of the world's largest medical center as well as the Manned Spacecraft Center. Houston became an international-level city.

Author Ralph Bivins experienced, lived and reported on Houston's rapid emergence as a world-class economic and culturally cosmopolitan urban area during the latter part of the last century and the first two decades of the 21st century.

The future of Houston seems boundless, increasing in speed and intensity. The energy sector surge brought on by the horizontal fracturing boom in oil and gas extraction as well as renewed growth in import/export activity through the Ports of Houston and Galveston plus the broader, more diversified businesses now finding homes in Houston provide the foundation for extended population and economic growth requiring even more creative land development scenarios. In *Houston 2020: America's Boom Town - An Extreme Close Up,* Ralph Bivins, provides a unique perspective on the history of Houston's development that illustrates some of the key aspects on what might be expected in the future growth of one of America's fastest-growing communities.

FOREWORD

By SANFORD W. CRINER, Vice Chairman CBRE

Houston has always been a real estate play. We started out that way: the original promotional sales flyer featured a bucolic alpine landscape to lure down unsuspecting Yankees. And we were founded at the same time as Chicago, but with none of their underlying economic justifications: *it was a real estate play*!

But the unforeseeable intervened with the convergence of the nearby discovery of oil at Spindletop in 1901, the devastation of Galveston – the leading economic center of the region – in the Great 1900 Storm, and the audacious decision of Houston leaders to dredge a small creek to create what is now the second largest port in the US – 50 miles from the coast. All at once, Houston became a center of business. It began to grow. Fast.

From 1900 to 1980, Houston grew at a compounded rate of just under 30% per decade, from 85th to 4th largest American city. In the last 3 decades, the average has dropped to 7.5%, still at or near the top of all large American cities. And passing Chicago to become the 3rd largest city has come to seem not just possible but inevitable.

So why has Houston continued to grow? Well, it's still the center of the international energy business. It's a low-cost, low-

FOREWORD

tax business environment. And you can do whatever you want with your real estate: we famously have no zoning laws.

But will low costs and limited regulations remain sufficient when quality of life is, for most employers, not only desirable but necessary? No. But that's OK, because Houston offers more.

Winston Churchill observed that "we shape our buildings; thereafter they shape us."

Houston has seen this play out through times when we built a tight, coherent, walkable urban fabric – largely up to World War II – and later during the post-war boom when we turned to a discontinuous, automobile-based model linked by freeways. This suburbanization of residential, retail, and office development reached its apotheosis in the overbuilding of the 1980's Oil Boom and we have been dealing with the residue of that event ever since.

Houston has finally escaped the gravitational pull of that era. The signs are visible everywhere: in the suburbs themselves, the most successful of which have become essentially small towns with walkable town centers, on-street parking, and sidewalk cafes; in the Bayou Greenways initiative, providing parks for all Houstonians and pedestrian and bike connectivity between all communities. In the world class office buildings being constructed and leased even when there remains a glut of buildings from the 80's. In the densification of the inner city and the internationally recognized restaurant scene which enriches and celebrates our diversity and thrives in this newly dense urban environment. Houston's most exciting era has begun.

With no natural boundaries, Houston will not and should not attempt to be like New York or San Francisco. Houston will remain Houston, but in a more humane, beautiful, and creative form to greet the challenge and the promise of the future.

PREFACE

Houston – the womb where I was conceived and the incubator that spat me out as a young man – faces a threatened future for the umpteenth time. The problems are bigger now, with sharper edges and deeper cuts leaving painful scars. But in many ways, today's challenges are the same as the ones faced by Houston in the past: managing growth, transportation, the economy and God-awful flooding that destroys property, stigmatizes neighborhoods and even steals the breath of life from our fellow Houstonians.

As the year 2020 emerges, Houston stands as the fourth-largest city in the nation, hurtling down a fast-growth track toward an uncertain destiny. The southeast Texas megalopolis pauses occasionally, providing a moment to consider the collateral damage amid its accomplishments. Then it stomps on the accelerator again. Like an old vinyl record that skips, Houston plays the same song again and again. With *Houston 2020: America's Boom Town – An Extreme Close Up,* together we look to the past to get a vision for the future. Will Houston falter under its own weight? Will Houston cut corners and take the cheap way out again? Will the developers of the city's real estate adapt to Houston's emerging realities or build the same old way in the same old places?

Houston is at a crossroads, the likes of which it has never seen before. And this time, it is imperative that Space City gets it right.

On one hand, promising opportunities present the chance to transform downtown and expand its boundaries into underutilized urban districts. Preservationists sail ahead with newly found tailwinds. Obsolete buildings in prime locations beg for redevelopment. Following an embarrassing rejection that left Houston off Amazon's short-list for its second headquarters, the city vigorously seeks economic development based on innovation and medical research. Houston's job growth is incredibly strong and home sales have been robust.

On the other hand, the darker pathway of Houston's possible destiny is sobering. No happy ending is guaranteed. Major cities – Detroit, Cleveland and New Orleans – have crumbled before, taken down by storm, corporate failure and the demise of industry. Houston floats like a massive raft in a deep canyon with choppy water underneath and unseen danger on the cliffs above. Whether it comes from port side or starboard, a loosened boulder will fly swiftly and a direct hit could sink the city. But Houston builds. It always builds.

Today, Houston's insatiable desire to build adds more skyscrapers to the skyline and more mid-rise office buildings to the suburbs, even while an oversupply of office space exists. New buildings attract corporate tenants that leave behind a negative wake of vacant office space, pressuring the owners of older properties. Fifty million square feet of office space lies vacant and no one knows for sure when – or if – it can be filled. Population growth and the demand for attainable housing pushes development farther into the suburbs and exurbs. In 2018, Howard Hughes Corporation opened The Woodlands Hills, a two thousand acre community near Willis, almost fifty miles from downtown Houston. As Houston spreads, commuting challenges mount for suburb dwellers. Commuter rail does not exist, leaving roadways as the sole solution. In the Inner Loop, residential expansion is vertical. High-rise apartment towers and condominiums rise in Downtown, Midtown and Uptown. High land costs dictate the contemporary blueprint: residential buildings must be tall to be profitable. More than five thousand urban high-rise apartment units are proposed or under construction. That does not count the scores of mid-rise apartment buildings coming up. No one constructs the smaller two-story, garden-style apartments of yore. Of course, the surge in close-in living units brings more density and more traffic, while urban Houstonians wait for the city's leadership to deliver mobility solutions. Questionable mobility projects abound – neutered by compromise, swayed by politics, and lacking the funding or leadership to develop outstanding, lasting transit answers.

The Houston economy? For decades, Houston leaders attempted to achieve a diversified economy without as much reliance on oil and gas. This initiative began in the 1980s when oil dropped below ten dollars a barrel about the same time the savings and loan institutions collapsed and Houston became the epicenter of realty foreclosures. In recent years, Houston's economy has diversified to a degree. The Texas Medical Center thrives. A proposed collaborative research park, with its phenomenal double-helix design element, could elevate the medical center to an even higher level of performance. Despite the successful efforts to diversify the local economy, the energy sector flexed its muscles with a throat-squeezing, three-year thrashing that began in 2014. Oil prices went into a deep decline and it was felt in Houston. Most of the Houston real estate markets performed fine, but the office sector took a hit. The Energy Corridor office market, which had been one of the nation's premier performers in 2013 with a Class A occupancy rate approaching 99 percent, soon became one of the worst submarkets in the US three years later. New buildings were completed and sat vacant for years, until Houston's office market improved significantly in the latter part of 2018. Questions remain. In a new era of energy, with fossil fuel opposition and the emergence of alternative energy sources, Houston leaders ponder how long will the city continue to call itself the "Energy Capital of the World?" How long will the Energy Corridor district maintain its title and status as the prime location for energy companies? Despite the diversity in the Houston economy, some truths never fail: when the price of West Texas Intermediate crude dips below forty dollars a barrel, there will be blood in the streets of Houston.

Then, there is the flooding. Hurricane Harvey, made landfall in Texas on August 25, 2017 and it stayed for days. Some places received fifty inches of rain. Some had more. The devastation was national news.

Harvey's damage and deaths made us weep. Harvey was the biggest flooding event in Houston's history, but it was not the only one. Other floods have walloped Houston in recent years and it seems like Houstonians can count on at least one major storm every year to drop ten inches of rain or more.

Some neighborhoods, after serving as great places to reside for decades, have been hit with multiple floods recently. Beloved but often-inundated homes are being elevated to rest on insanely tall foundations, like stilt-supported beach houses on Galveston Island. Bulldozers flatten other houses along flood-prone streets. City leaders search for answers to the riddle of growth: How can suburban construction expand without exacerbating flooding downstream in the Inner Loop? The images of repeated flooding cast a shadow over Houston's reputation and threaten to derail attempts to attract new businesses. Hurricane Harvey delivered a hard gut punch to Houston, but no one expects the city to surrender.

This is Houston – a city that overcomes floods. It's a city that erected the world's first air-conditioned domed stadium. It's a city that created the world's largest medical center and a massive inland port fifty miles from the coast. For several consecutive

PREFACE

years, Houston has ranked Number Two in the nation, behind only Dallas-Fort Worth, in single-family housing construction. Houston has been a national leader in job growth and population gains, with 94,417 new Houstonians arriving in 2017, says the latest annual census report. The Houston metropolitan area is home to 6,892,437 people with a richly diverse ethnic composition. Houston is an American boomtown. Now more than ever, it deserves a careful examination, a dissection of its downtown and real estate activity centers, a fresh spotlight on its prime projects.

Houston deserves an extremely close-up look at its soul.

– *Ralph Bivins*

1
THE SOUL OF HOUSTON

HOUSTON IS SPEEDING toward a turning point. The population of Greater Houston is expected to hit 10 million by 2040. No one expects the growth to come easy. Some expect the growing pains to be excruciating, even deadly.

Optimistic Houstonians embrace the hope that answers can be developed for the big questions facing the city's leaders. Is Houston going to be the city that addressed the flooding crisis head-on and solved its massive drainage problems? Is Houston going to be the city that solved mobility issues in a new way, casting aside the notions of former leadership that more roadways and wider freeways can suffice as the universal Band-Aid for whatever ails the city? Yes, the optimists say, attainable housing can be developed for the incoming generation without requiring Houstonians to endure two-hour commutes.

The skeptic draws a darker picture of the future. Houston swells into obesity, an insatiable monster extending its freeway tentacles further and further into the exurbs. Ruthless expansion lies deep in its DNA, requiring the city to consume more of the Texas coastal prairie. Houston must expand. The skeptics believe the adherents of the growth cult will sacrifice anyone and anything to reach their goal and their common daily prayer is to surpass Chicago to become the nation's third largest city. Even if the growth is choking the interior of the metropolis and pinching closed the city's arteries of mobility, Houston must expand. Wild suburban growth and its hardened impenetrable pavement drown the heart of the mother city in floodwaters, scuttle her, and take her to the bottom.

The decisions offer little leeway for delay. Climate change makes the eight-inch rainstorm a fairly common event these days. Economic growth lures people to Houston where more than one thousand new jobs are created every week. The city is poised at the crossroads and a wrong turn could sink the Bayou City.

With the threats demanding immediate action, perhaps the city's leadership should begin with meditation focused on the city's underpinnings — the Soul of Houston, the sanctuary at the headwaters of civic identity. It's not hard to find. Finding the Soul of Houston requires no arduous pilgrimage. It's housed in a landmark.

Rarely does a building embody the true culture of a city. Rarely does a building owe its existence to the prevailing ethos of a community — an ambitious project in a can-do city. It can be hard to find a tangible front door to the inner spirit of a metropolis. But sometimes a city's soul can be located and sometimes, the date it reached critical mass can be pinpointed exactly. It was January 3, 1962 — the date of a publicity stunt.

It started with a bang.

Instead of using shovels like a normal groundbreaking, men fired Colt .45 revolvers into the ground, signaling the beginning of construction of what would become one of the most famous structures in the world.

The city was Houston, a metropolitan region on the rise as it earned its status as the Energy Capital of the World. The state was Texas, where everything is bigger. And the project was the Astrodome, soon to be the world's largest room. Within a year after opening in 1965, the Astrodome would be America's third-most-popular man-made tourist attraction — only the Golden Gate Bridge and Mount Rushmore drew more visitors. People would pay a dollar just for a tour of the empty stadium — no ballgame required.

Dubbed the "The Eighth Wonder of the World," it was an impressive engineering feat — the world's first domed stadium — setting the bar for copycat stadiums that would follow. The Astrodome would be the home of the Houston Astros — the city's Major League Baseball team, which originally was called the Colt .45s. The Dome housed the Houston Oilers, Houston's NFL franchise — and the Houston Livestock Show and Rodeo, as well as a variety of events from basketball to bullfights. The Supremes were the first act to perform, opening for Judy Garland before a sold-out crowd that paid as little as one dollar, up to the premium ticket price of seven dollars and fifty cents for tickets. Elvis Presley, Evel Knievel, Muhammad Ali, and evangelist Billy Graham all filled the forty-two-thousand cushioned seats at the Dome. (With biblical-like authority, the Rev. Graham was featured in Dome advertisements proclaiming, "This is, in truth, one of the great wonders of the world.")

In 1968, a contest promoted as the Game of the Century — a basketball game between the University of Houston Cougars and the UCLA Bruins was played on the floor of the Astrodome. It was the first NCAA regular season game to be broadcast nationally in prime time.

Enthralled with the scope and vision of the place, Hollywood even produced a movie staged in the stadium — Director Robert Altman's 1970s experimental comedy *Brewster McCloud* about a young outsider who lives in a fallout shelter at the Dome, where he was building a pair of wings, so he could fly. As the role of women in the changing nation was evolving, the publicity-drenched Battle of the Sexes tennis match between Bobby Riggs and Billie Jean King was presented at the Dome in 1973. Twenty years later, the Republican National Convention met under its big roof to anoint George H.W. Bush and running mate Dan

Quayle. Over the years, the Dome hosted music legends including Bob Dylan, Frank Sinatra, Aretha Franklin, and the Rolling Stones.

"People who don't know much about Houston know the Astrodome," says Houston Realtor Minnette Boesel, a leader in preservation for the city for decades. "The Astrodome and the Alamo are the two most well-known Texas architectural landmarks that people recognize. The Astrodome is a symbol of Houston's bravado and can-do spirit throughout the world. It was the first of its kind. How lucky are we to have it in Houston — and that it still exists. Most cities that build new stadiums tear the old ones down. Fortunately, that didn't happen here."

The Dome is more than a stadium. It's an American innovation credited as the vision of the late Roy Hofheinz, a former Houston mayor and a world-class huckster who would eventually buy the Ringling Bros. and Barnum & Bailey Circus.

Stephen Fox, architectural historian and a lecturer at the Rice School of Architecture and the Gerald D. Hines College of Architecture at the University of Houston, adds that the Astrodome is a historically significant work of engineering design. "It was the first of its kind: an enclosed, air-conditioned sports arena," Fox explains. "Houston identifies with the Astrodome. It is a site of collective memory. Houstonians recognize what a remarkable twentieth century landmark they possess in the Astrodome and that it should be preserved, rehabilitated, and re-used."

For many people in the city and elsewhere, the Astrodome **IS** Houston — central to its identity and a monument to an era of grand ambition for Houston, the nation's fourth largest city. Architect Louis H. Skidmore Jr., a consultant to global design firm Skidmore, Owings and Merrill, currently with Cooke + Skidmore Consulting Corp., notes the Astrodome had a tremendous effect on the psyche of Houston. "The Astrodome gave us so much self-confidence that we felt we could build and dream big — anything was possible," says Skidmore, a member of advisory board of Preservation Houston. "After all, the Astrodome was such an odd idea for the times — an indoor sports stadium. Today, it seems natural. But sixty years ago, it was a simple yet radical design and an example of the city's 'can-do' spirit!"

Three decades before the Astrodome was designed, air-conditioning pioneer Willis Carrier articulated his vision for a future where people would reside under transparent domes, eliminating inclement weather as a messy factor in daily life. Hofheinz — many Houstonians just called him "The Judge" — embraced Carrier's vision and worked to create an air-conditioned, built environment. Defending the idea in the early stages, observers said, Hofheinz corralled the naysayers like a relentless quarter horse herding cattle into a rodeo chute.

As the persistent Judge marched ahead to will the stadium into existence, the Astrodome earned a reputation for over-achievement and an unwavering tenacity. Years before construction started — and several years before the Civil Rights Act of 1964 – Hofheinz gathered early support from the African-American community by promising the Dome would be fully integrated from the beginning. No hurdle too high. No challenge too great.

The Dome was built in the midst of Houston's feverish pursuit of the impossible. Innovation was in the city's air in the 1960s and Houstonians breathed it deeply. NASA chose Houston as headquarters for the Manned Spacecraft Center, and space heroes like John Glenn moved to town. The Space Race with the Russians was real and NASA scientists in Houston hurried to complete the objective voiced by President John F. Kennedy at a speech at Rice University Stadium in 1962: The nation must put a man on the moon before the end of the decade.

Just a couple of miles from the Dome, physicians at the Texas Medical Center were in their own race, pioneering methods for heart transplant surgery and developing the artificial heart. With competing efforts that would be called a feud, two brilliant heart surgeons — Dr. Denton Cooley and Dr. Michael DeBakey — were making cardiovascular history. Cooley performed the world's first artificial heart transplant in Houston in 1969.

Nothing seemed impossible in Space City. It was the 1960s and Houston pioneered on three frontiers: cardiac treatment discoveries, NASA's space exploration, and the development of the world's first air-conditioned domed stadium.

For years, Houston's economic engine has been driven by the energy industry and medicine, says architect John Cryer III, board emeritus of Page Southerland Page Inc. and immediate past president of Preservation Houston. "Houston energy leaders have worked all over the world and, as a result, have built relationships with local governments and people," says Cryer. "There are multiculture families and multicultural business skills and relationships. We have become a melting pot linked together through business and science. There is no other city that can compare to the homogenized spirit of Houston. As a result, Houston will be the city that becomes iconic on the national stage as one that broke down barriers. The Astrodome represented the 'bigger than life' and 'can do anything' culture of the city."

Former Houston Mayor Bill White — who led Houston from 2006 to 2010 and opened the Astrodome to residents of New Orleans following Hurricane Katrina — adds that Houston is a city of doers and not complainers. "By and large, most people moved here from somewhere else in order to work," White explains. "We have a large number of hardworking, skilled, first- and second-generation Americans who are performing jobs ranging from department heads at Baylor College of Medicine to skilled carpenters, and who are taking a risk in a new country. That's one of the things that contributes to the grit of Houston."

The Dome showed Houston's chutzpah at its peak. The Astrodome was one of the first stadiums to have fifty-three luxury suites called Skyboxes. In centerfield was a two-million-dollar, 474-foot-long scoreboard, a Texas-size spectacular display. The scoreboard entertained crowds even when the baseball team was mired in its losing ways. When the Astros hit a homer, the giant scoreboard lit up to depict a pyrotechnic display. Cowboys emerged, bullets ricocheted, an angry snorting bull erupted with US and Texas flags attached to its electronic horns. If the opposing team happened to hit a home run, the scoreboard flashed "Tilt."

The Dome was originally known as the Harris County Domed Stadium, but the clunky title faded fast and Houstonians soon called it by a more noble name that endured: "The Astrodome." In an era when Gunsmoke and Bonanza were top television shows, the Colt .45s were a popular name for the baseball team, which played its first game in 1962. But new American heroes emerged — space explorers. So Hofheinz embraced the new Space Age theme. The Colt .45s were shelved; their inferior little stadium would be replaced, dismantled, and eventually shipped to a minor league team in Mexico. The new team was the Astros, and Hofheinz launched the space theme with full vigor. The stadium's field crews were dressed in space-suit costumes and the female ushers were called the Spacettes. While NASA was innovating at the new Johnson Space Center on the southeast side of town, Hofheinz unleashed his marketing genius on the ball club with the astronaut theme and its new stadium. Houston was called "Space City" and it had a baseball park that matched.

When it opened in 1965, the Dome was a marvel of mechanical engineering with an ultraviolet-ray smoke detector for checking visibility and a weather station on the roof that fed data to a computer that kept the temperature a constant 72 degrees, considered quite balmy in a city where the average August high is well over 90. The air conditioning itself was a new-fangled marvel of cooling power with the ability to blow chilled air 300 feet.

The Dome was eighteen stories above the playing field and

consisted of 4,596 Lucite panels — skylights that were designed to allow the natural grass playing field to grow. However, the translucent panels soon presented a problem. During afternoon games outfielders were blinded by the sunlight when they went to catch fly balls. Thirty percent of the roof panels then were coated with paint to reduce the glare. When the natural grass playing field died due to the lack of sunlight, a new type of turf — a green surface of nylon grass — was created with Monsanto. Astroturf, another Houston Dome innovation, became a staple at stadiums throughout the country, even at regular outdoor stadiums without roofs. Houston's innovative spirit gave birth to plastic grass.

Always known for putting on a good show, Houston and Hofheinz didn't disappoint on the Astrodome's opening night. The April 9, 1965, exhibition baseball game pitted the Houston Astros against the New York Yankees and featured twenty-one astronauts throwing out the first twenty one pitches. The sellout crowd honored John Young and Gus Grissom, who had become the first American astronaut pair in space. President Lyndon Baines Johnson and Texas Governor John Connally were pampered in the opulent presidential suite featuring priceless Louis XIV furniture. On the field, Yankee superstar Mickey Mantle baptized the place that night by hitting the Dome's first homer.

Constructing the Astrodome was not merely erecting a building; it was creating a vision of the future. Initially, Hofheinz's idea was based upon meeting a need: If Houston was ever going to get a major league baseball team, an indoor stadium was required. Houston's Equator-like heat and mosquito invasions had always tamped down the crowds at outdoor events. Ever the entrepreneur, Hofheinz aspired for much more than a baseball facility. He envisioned a venue for a whole host of activities that could be much more enjoyable under a dome in a climate-controlled environment. He endured the taunts of skeptics, but his vision, foresight and tenacity changed the world of sports and entertainment.

The Astrodome continued to be the soul of Houston for decades. But after some thirty years, the city seemed to be losing its soul. The Greek philosopher Aristotle once said, "Memory is the scribe to the soul." Eventually, Houstonians started forgetting the Dome's meaning. The memory of the Astrodome started to fade. The soul lost touch with the memory. A glitzier, larger, and more profitable stadium was a must, they said. The Astrodome's glory days lasted until the dawn of the twenty-first century. The Dome closed after the 1999 baseball season and the Astros moved to the new Enron Field (now called Minute Maid Park) in downtown. Soon, the Dome sat forlorn in the shadow of the hulking new Houston Texans (NFL) facility — the NRG Stadium. The Dome was less than 40 years old, but this was a disposable world and the owners of professional sports teams demanded newness.

The Astrodome just sat empty and unwanted — until Hurricane Katrina hit New Orleans in 2005. In one final, valiant act of usefulness the Astrodome reopened as a shelter for evacuees who arrived by the busload. Cots, food, clothing, and a roof overhead provided shelter for thousands displaced by catastrophic flooding. Americans had been horrified with days of television images of death and destruction and masses of people seeking shelter in the grim New Orleans Superdome, dubbed the "shelter of last resort." The evacuees, with no place else to turn, headed for Houston's Dome. With legendary operational efficiency and compassion, Mayor Bill White, according to *Texas Monthly*, welcomed the storm's victims, citing scripture from the New Testament's Book of Matthew: "For I was hungry and you fed me. I was a stranger and you took me in." Various helpers and Houston-based counselors and pastors came to the Dome to deliver emotional and physical comfort. While city leaders in Dallas complained they were overwhelmed by evacuees, Houston leadership opened the

Dome to tens of thousands, plus tens of thousands more in other venues. And Houston officials — led by Mayor White, the greatest municipal field general the city has ever seen — kept the doors open to assist even more evacuees — a total of some 250,000. Once again, the Dome was innovating, this time creating ways to show compassion when the need was massive. The grande dame of stadiums had dusted herself off and spread her wings to provide shelter for the masses. It was the Dome's finest hour.

After the Katrina crisis had passed, days of doubt began hovering over the Dome. The wrecking ball crowd began mumbling.

In 2008, the city's fire marshal closed the building and declared it unsafe for occupancy. Two years later, a study estimated that demolishing the "Eighth Wonder of the World" would cost $128 million, an option that many officials and Houstonians had been reluctant to consider. A proposed solution came and went in 2013, when voters rejected a referendum that would have authorized up to $217 million in bonds to turn the Astrodome into a giant convention and event center.

Time was not on the Astrodome's side. The stadium seemed on course to be demolished. In 2016, nearly all of the interior fixtures including the seats were stripped from the stadium. Most of the excitement generated by the Astrodome in the 1960s was forgotten as the world's largest room sat empty. Talk of tearing down the stadium rumbled louder. The naysayers advocated strongly for demolition. Would it be a catastrophe if the Dome were razed? An immense tragedy, the Save the Dome crowd said, because that would be destroying something that was a prototype and that is intimately connected to the emotional experiences of generations of Houstonians. Erasing the memory of the Astrodome would impoverish Houston and the culture of the city.

Harris County's top elected official, County Judge Ed Emmett, wasn't going to let that happen on his watch. Emmett led the charge for saving the Astrodome, citing one major reason: It was paid for.

"Some people have emotional reasons for saving it, but truth of it is that as Harris County Judge, I view it as a fully paid asset. It belongs to the taxpayers and it is very useful. What is lost on most people is that the Astrodome is part of the NRG complex and the county has a contract to maintain the entire complex. Since we really only have property tax revenue here in Harris County, we view the Dome as a revenue source – nine acres of covered, rentable space is a valuable asset. With the Astrodome, you've got an attraction and a revenue source. It's a big plus for the Houston Livestock Show and Rodeo, the largest livestock exhibition and rodeo in the world."

Emmett's reasoning carried the day. In February 2018, Harris County commissioners approved a $105 million redevelopment of the Astrodome including raising the ground level two floors to create two levels of underground parking — some 1,400 spaces — that can also be used for football games, conferences, and festivals. Construction is expected to be complete by February 2020, although Judge Emmett was defeated in his re-election bid in November 2018.

"The Astrodome is a resource that benefits the community," says Minnette Boesel, the preservationist. "You could have concerts there, or festivals, or even fund-raisers. You could have the world's largest indoor yoga class. The Texans and the Rodeo are interested in using the structure. It's a symbol of the world."

In partnership with the Harris County Sports and Convention Corporation, the Astrodome Conservancy under Chair Phoebe Tudor scheduled an open house at the Astrodome in April 2018 for Houstonians. It was a unique event and no one knew what to expect. "We had 25,000 tickets that went online at

10 a.m., and by 11:45 a.m., the 25,000 tickets were gone," says Boesel. "We couldn't believe it. People were still streaming through the Astrodome at 10:30 at night, which just shows how much people care about the Astrodome."

People will have many more years to appreciate the significance of the historic structure. The Astrodome — an accomplishment in engineering that symbolizes Houston's undefeatable spirit — will be used for years to come. Buildings in Europe stand for centuries. Over the years, Houston's leaders have been too quick to demolish its history. The drive to save the Dome changed all that.

The first domed stadium, the first word heard from the moon, the first artificial heart surgery — all were achieved thanks to Houston's spirit. Innovation, entrepreneurship, and unlimited opportunity – that's what Space City is about. Houston is the gutsy city with no zoning and no limits. The city where success is about your ability, hard work and guts — not about your social pedigree or Ivy League diploma.

Former Mayor Bill White said the city is a work in progress.

"Every generation has some opportunity and responsibility of taking Houston in a new direction. These are question marks but I'm optimistic about Houston's future. We have the highest concentration of engineers in the country, because of our legacy of leadership in the energy industry. We have a relatively low cost of living and a very deep, small-business community with a lot of entrepreneurs. One of my predecessors noted there are so many resilient entrepreneurs in Houston because our traditional real estate and oil and gas industries are cyclical. Many of our successful business leaders are the same people who at some time in their careers had to reorganize their debt or who had been wiped out financially before. I think Houston has more resilience because of our history. Houstonians view our diversity of background, cultures, and religions as our strengths. It makes us hospitable to multi-cultural experiences."

— BILL WHITE, FORMER HOUSTON MAYOR

Saving the Dome — it was recognized as a protected antiquities landmark by the Texas Historical Commission in 2017 — represented a huge victory for preservation. It was a rare win in a city where bulldozers have been victorious most of the time. The obituary list is long: The 1949-vintage Shamrock Hotel, an 1,100-room property that was the biggest hotel built in the US in the post-war 1940s, is long gone. The eighteen-story Prudential Building, built in 1952 as the city's first office tower located outside downtown, was demolished in 2012 and its site remained vacant land for years thereafter. Downtown's ornate movie palaces of the 1920s — including the Majestic, Loews State, and the Metropolitan theaters — were swept away. Old Houston neighborhoods lose character as old bungalows and low-slung ranch-style houses are destroyed and replaced with bigger new houses often grossly oversized for their lots.

Progress — however it is defined — cannot be stopped. Wrecking balls are powerful. Perhaps, the Astrodome is starting a winning streak for preservation in Space City. Perhaps the Dome's rebirth will teach Houstonians that the rewards for preserving history can be rich. Old is not bad.

2

THREE WISE MEN: LESSONS LEARNED

ONE YOUNG HOUSTONIAN started his business because his boss refused to give him a promised bonus. In doing so, he turned a stodgy industry on its head. Forty-two years later, the Houston-based company is the nation's largest privately held homebuilder with annual revenues of $2 billion dollars.

Another individual had an idea for a different kind of real estate company that would create a unique culture where customers AND employees came first. At this innovative Bayou City-headquartered firm, employees are highly valued assets.

The third was an entrepreneur who wanted to change the way buildings were constructed by making them more efficient — more than four decades before other developers followed suit. He also decided to team up with the world's most creative "starchitects" to build eye-dropping corporate headquarters for companies around the world, beginning the era of the "star architect."

All three started out with a dream and passion for hard work. All three turned their dreams into billion-dollar companies in Houston. And all three — David Weekley, chairman of David Weekley Homes; Ric Campo, chief executive officer of multi-family real estate firm Camden Property Trust; and Gerald D.

Hines, the founder and chairman of privately held global real estate company Hines — credit the city with a large part of their success.

"In Houston, if you have a good idea, and work hard, the capital will come to you," says Campo. "In Houston, it doesn't matter if you are a member of the River Oaks Country Club or your father or grandfather was a member. Houston is a welcoming place for all, has grown with no social barriers and is one of the most diverse cities in America. We don't have problems like they do in places like Ferguson. We get along with each other and we don't care about your religion, color, or where you are from. We care about whether you can get it done. Possibly because we are a young city, with no barrier to entry, Houston has a social system that's not about the college you attended or whether you were born in the blue-blood social register."

DAVID WEEKLEY HOMES

Weekley — who was born and raised in Houston — echoes Camden's analysis: "Houston's got an entrepreneurial spirit. It doesn't matter what your name is or where you came from or if you are rich or poor. If you are able to come up with an idea and meet a market, people in Houston welcome you and encourage your success."

Consider David Weekley. With 2018 revenues of more than two billion dollars, David Weekley Homes is the largest privately held home builder in America. David Weekley started the company in 1976 when he was twenty-three years old. "I was working for another home builder in Houston. I liked the company and I learned a lot," recalls Weekley. "I was leading my own team, building new homes in a subdivision of Houston. We did well, and I earned a bonus. But the company wanted to give me a company car instead. It was a matter of principle. I went to see the company president who told me I had a bad attitude and take a hike. I left."

Weekley had developed a passion for building quality homes, though, and wanted to remain in the industry. "My brother Dick had tremendous confidence in me and he risked everything to get a line of credit for us. We started David Weekley Homes and never looked back. Our 'world headquarters' in the beginning was a construction trailer in the middle of a field. Then we moved to a house garage, then into a house, followed by a warehouse. Now we have our own office building in the Galleria area of Houston."

What was the key to David Weekley Homes' success? "From the beginning, we paid attention to design. We wanted to give our customers what they wanted, not dictate what they must buy," he explains. "I started to ask questions about the design of other model homes. Why were there only a few windows? Why were the ceilings only eight feet high? We created our brand promise around design, choice, and service. We paid close attention to home design; today we have one hundred architects and designers on our staff. Design is a key component of what to do. Other builders said, 'take it my way' but we would build homes the way customers wanted."

Weekley offered a rich array of options that blurred the line between custom homes and production ones. "We also made a determination that the people we hired would drive the business and their interaction with customers would result in our success," says Weekley. "Home building is a rough-and-tumble business. But if you take care of your people, they will take great care of your customers. In these days of social media and the Internet, great customer service pays great dividends. A third of our sales now are from referrals and a third of our new buyers see our great customer ratings on the web. Our success has been forty-two years in the making. One of our company's values is to continue to improve. Our team is driven to excellence. We are constantly changing and moving to what our customers' needs are. We don't stay static. We move and change as our markets move and change. We worked hard, and we were rewarded for our people-first culture when we were named to Fortune magazine's '100 Best Companies to Work For' — twelve times."

Weekley thought about taking the company public in the early 1990s but made a firm decision to remain private. "As a private company, we're not beholden to quarterly earnings forecasts for Wall Street," he continues. "Being private allows us to meet the needs of our customers and our team and our community. We also give out twenty percent of our earnings to area nonprofits each year. Giving back is a core belief of ours. If we were a public company, we wouldn't be able to do that to the same degree."

David Weekley Homes' reputation for taking care of its customers and its hometown was further enhanced after Hurricane Harvey: Weekley was not aware of any of the homes the company built over the past forty years that flooded. True to its mission of helping the community, the David Weekley Family Foundation committed one million dollars to BuildAidHouston.org, a new nonprofit initiative providing Houston homeowners with much-needed home repairs at cost following the devastation from Hurricane Harvey.

"Houston is a great place and we want to be a good corporate citizen," says Weekley. "Houston is a fantastic city to live in and do business in."

CAMDEN PROPERTY TRUST

California native Ric Campo moved to Houston in 1976 when his father opened a short-lived restaurant in the city. Initially a chemistry major who changed to accounting, Campo went to work at Century Development Corp. of Houston. After a decade, he and his partner Keith Oden led a leveraged buyout of the division that morphed into Camden. The pair steadily built up Camden's portfolio through acquisitions and development. Today, Houston-based Camden owns interests in more than 160 properties with more than

55,000 apartment homes across the United States. But Campo and Oden didn't just want to create another real estate firm. They sought to build a company with its own corporate culture. The name "Camden" was derived from a combination of their last names.

"We worked hard. We had a good idea and capital formed around Camden," said Campo. "We figured out what we want to do and how to get bigger. The first thing was recruiting the best and brightest and give them the resources and authority to achieve goals and then get out of their way. We believe in the interaction of a winning team. Why does one team win, and another doesn't? It's about the chemistry and culture. We spend a lot of time focusing on how to build, maintain, and nurture our culture. We want our team to have the spirit and energy that continually drives to win."

Thus, it's no surprise that for eleven years running, the company has been named by Fortune Magazine as one of the "100 Best Companies to Work For" in America.

Campo frequently dons a standard Camden maintenance man shirt — with a patch that says "Ric" — when he makes appearances at company meetings. He says it helps him connect with employees and shows his respect for the Camden workers in the field, and all of the firm's 1,600 employees.

Camden, Campo says, just operates differently. When the firm restructured a joint venture a few years ago resulting in a one-hundred-million-dollar profit, Camden and Oden decided to distribute 10 percent of that windfall to employees. But they didn't want to just deposit the bonus in their employees' bank accounts. They wanted their team "feel" the moment by having an actual check in their hands, so Camden cut real checks for each and every employee. The checks were sent to every Camden location in large boxes with instructions that the packages were not to be opened until a certain day and a specific time. Camden then scheduled a company-wide conference call and the bonus was distributed in celebratory unison. All employees received a check of at least one thousand dollars, depending on the years with the company.

Camden's executive suite also operates differently from most real estate concerns. Campo and Oden have been partners for more than three decades and continue to be excited about working with each other. "You have to keep adapting to change and you have to have mutual respect for each other," says Campo, who is usually the public face of Camden, a publicly traded real estate investment trust, or REIT. "That's the thing that has kept us together. We can disagree vehemently, but we don't go after each other's throats. We just move on to the next topic. It's an issue of fairness. You respect another person's opinion. You can argue and fight, but it doesn't mean that you hate their guts. We never fight over an issue that could become a defining moment."

Both have very different operating styles, Campo adds, and it's all about balance. Campo jokes that he's the gas while Oden is the brakes. "We have conflict and some heated debates, but then we get back on the same page and we get the things we need to get done."

HINES

As a boy growing up in Gary, Indiana, Gerald D. Hines remembers sitting out on his back porch making model airplanes.

"I think I've always enjoyed building whether it was carpentry or model airplanes," Hines said when he was honored by the National Building Museum in Washington, D.C. "That has always been a creative part of my life and I needed to express it in another way when I became an adult."

Over the ensuing eight decades, Hines has done exactly that. The late US President George H.W. Bush at the same ceremony noted that Hines provided distinctive architecture to cities around the world, particularly Houston. "Gerald Hines envisioned Houston as a city of beautiful buildings, a truly quality built environment," continued Bush. "He enlisted the aid of great architects to produce buildings that made people proud and that raised the quality of other developers."

That was an understatement. Hines has changed the face of Houston and other cities with iconic creations such as the Big Apple's pinkish, oval-shaped "Lipstick Building" with one of his favorite architects, Philip Johnson, and Frank Gehry's DZ Bank building in Berlin that sports an interior courtyard of a massive, titanium, morphing form.

But it is the early day Houston projects that Hines tackled early in his career, that mean the most to him, the developer said in an email in late 2018. "My favorite projects will always be our early ones in Houston — One Shell Plaza, Pennzoil Place, and The Galleria. Pennzoil Place really put us on the map when we completed it in 1975. The unique design came from architects Philip Johnson and John Burgee. No one had ever put two buildings on one city block before. Ada Louise Huxtable (the architecture critic at The New York Times) named Pennzoil 'Building of the Decade.' That was an exciting time for our firm."

Today, the organization that Gerald D. Hines began in 1957 is one of the largest real estate organizations in the world. The privately owned global real estate investment, development, and management firm, has a presence in two hundred and seven cities in twenty-four countries with $116.4 billion of assets under management — including $64 billion for which Hines provides fiduciary investment management services and $52.4 billion for which Hines provides third-party property-level services, according to the company.

Hines has more than a hundred developments currently underway around the world, and historically, has developed, redeveloped, or acquired 1,319 properties, totaling more than 431 million square feet. The firm's current property and asset management portfolio includes 527 properties, representing more than 224 million square feet. That's a far cry from building model airplanes on the back porch.

A mechanical engineer by trade, Hines was a different kind of developer from the very beginning. Architects said he was the ideal client: committed to striving for the best possible design, concerned with the building process from beginning to end, not afraid of innovation, mindful of even small issues. As part of Hines' ninetieth birthday celebration in 2015, some of the world's leading architects came to Houston for the Hines Architectural Forum: A Conversation with Gerald D. Hines and the Living Legends of Architecture. Panelists included Frank Gehry, Cesar Pelli, Robert A.M. Stern, Henry N. Cobb, Jon Pickard, and John Burgee, the late Philip Johnson's design partner. Hines pushed great architecture into the marketplace, proving that outstanding buildings can command higher rents. When it became evident that great design translated into greater profit, capitalist developers followed suit.

As an engineer, Hines understood that it was easy to create a great building with an expensive price tag. It was much more difficult to plan a great building at a *competitive* price. The difference was all in the details. And Gerald Hines delved into the details of the company's buildings. He had the knowledge, effort, and discipline to do this, understanding that a significant amount of savings comes from building a high-quality structure at the outset. In that way, the finished product not only operates more efficiently, but increases value over the years and can be retrofitted easier in the future. Hines ruined many suits crawling through the heating and ventilation ducts to show off the systems to clients. And even into the digital age, he usually carried a reminder from his engineering courses at Purdue — an old-school slide rule so he could make quick calculations.

During economic downturns such as the oil bust that began in 2014, the Hines organization continued to build quality buildings, such as 609 Main at Texas in downtown Houston. The forty-eight-story, one-million-square-foot office tower designed by the Pickard Chilton architecture firm and topped with a diagonal crown was a new landmark for the city's skyline. "The building, with rooftop gardens, resort-level finishes in common areas and the latest in technology, including an advanced ten-million-dollar air conditioning system, could re-define the characteristics of Class AA space in Houston," said Realty News Report.

Hines imprinted lasting marks on the Houston skyline and in dozens of cities around the world with a portfolio that includes office towers, hotels, museums, retail centers, land developments, residential towers, seniors housing, and structures for government, medicine, education, and sports. The legacy also includes the Gerald D. Hines College of Architecture and Design at the University of Houston.

When asked, as 2018 came to a close, if he has any advice for young developers breaking into the business today,. Hines offered these words of wisdom: "Develop quality products and look for projects that show imagination. Also, it's important to treat tenants with great respect and integrity.

"Finally, I would say always do more than you promise."

3
THE RESILIENT CITY

THE IMAGES on the television screens carried a payload of emotional weight. A little family waded out of a barrio in waist-high brown water and everyone knew they lost everything they had, which wasn't much to begin with. Volunteers in small boats — piloted by men who previously had been labeled "rednecks" by suddenly appreciative city dwellers — ventured off into flooded streets and overflowing bayous to rescue people from fast-rising water.

The downtown Theater District, where the ballet, opera and theater companies performed, was inundated; its huge inventory of props and costumes, including five hundred wigs, were ruined. Along Buffalo Bayou, flood waters poured into the broadcast studios of KHOU-TV, forcing the CBS affiliate to evacuate the building.

Across Houston, sacred buildings and beloved homes were in deep, filthy water.

The slogan "Houston Strong" emerged as rain finally subsided and people began to assess the damage, even though many homes would have standing water inside for days after the storm eased.

Remaining "strong" was no easy task. Not for people who

lost all their family photos. Not for the small business owner with inadequate insurance. Not for the widower who struggles — and often fails — to cope with the pain of compounded loss.

Not for the fiction writer who saved his latest manuscript from fast-rising water by yanking the memory card out of his computer. His heavily damaged home has been sold, but he mourns losing four hundred books from a personal library that defined his world.

Remaining "Houston Strong" was not easy for the people who were acquainted with Jim Simmon, a retired 63-year-old journalist who reportedly had some early-onset memory issues. As Harvey was winding down, Simmon left his Montrose area home and got turned around. He was missing for two weeks after the hurricane. Finally, his body was found twenty miles from his home in a Fort Bend County sand pit, an apparent drowning victim.

When schools finally reopened in nearby Dickinson, some two weeks after the storm had passed, another sad story was reported. On the first day of school, more than a dozen students showed up for class with no shoes, barefoot because their families — in the post-hurricane crisis — lacked the wherewithal to dress them.

The emotional weight was heavy in Houston. Even men who normally keep their feelings locked behind heavy coats of armor felt the loss when they were alone, in private.

The road to rebound has been long. Volunteers came from around the country to tear out wet drywall and remove soggy furniture. Huge mountains of trash — soaked carpets, mattresses, and dead appliances — lined miles of curbs for weeks. But complaining was minimal because everyone knew that trash pickup of this magnitude was no overnight matter. Although great progress came, more than a year after Hurricane Harvey made landfall in August 2017, hundreds of properties still awaited repairs. People without flood insurance could not afford to rebuild. Labor was hard to find. Construction was slow. Some people completed the partial repairs that they could afford and lived in unfinished houses with bare lumber uncovered by drywall. Some homeowners went through the expensive process of elevating their home, jacking them upward, six feet or more in most cases, to rest on new, higher foundations. Charity organizations remained in Houston for over a year, their volunteer crews rebuilding houses for unfortunate flood victims.

Houston may have been down, but it's not out, according to the city's mayor.

> Resiliency is in Houston's DNA. The city has bounced back countless times — from oil busts, other economic shocks, hurricanes, and floods. We are a changed city, having been through hell and high water as a unified community. It's been not just our hope, but also our goal — to which we have given a lot of sweat equity — to change our city into one that is more resilient in the next storm. Fortunately, we are making progress, one ordinance, federal funding mechanism, bayou widening, and home elevation at a time.
>
> — HOUSTON MAYOR SYLVESTER TURNER

In Houston, Hurricane Harvey was not noted for its wild winds. It was a rainstorm, the likes of which the nation has never seen before.

The rain began like it often does in Houston, in fitful starts followed by unimaginable intensity.

Continuing for days, the deluge turned roads into rivers across Houston. By the time the skies cleared, Hurricane Harvey had deposited more than forty inches of rain over ninety-six hours during the last week in August of 2017. Some places registered more than 50 inches. By measuring how much the earth had been compressed, scientists calculated that the record-breaking storm has dropped thirty-four trillion gallons of water on the state — equivalent to filling twenty-six thousand New Orleans Superdomes.

Harvey was the most significant tropical cyclone rainfall event since reliable rainfall records began around the 1880s, according to the National Hurricane Center. The storm directly killed at least sixty-eight people, all of them in Texas, and indirectly killed some thirty-five more. It was the most damaging storm in US history, causing about $125 billion in damage, reported the National Oceanic and Atmospheric Administration. More than 150,000 homes were flooded, as well as hundreds of businesses. The storm destroyed more than 300,000 vehicles in Houston, according to media reports.

The Harris County Flood Control District estimated 70 percent of Harris County, where Houston is located, was flooded by at least 1.5 feet of water, a total of a trillion gallons.

Beyond the devastation, the images of Harvey that most people around the globe remember are that of neighbor helping neighbor, of individuals with pickup trucks pulling boats and trailers driving to Houston to help rescue residents, and of the indelible, undefeatable spirit of Houstonians during a time of extreme hardship.

"The city and the people of the area responded to Harvey with fortitude and resilience," said Bill White, Houston's sixtieth mayor, serving from 2004 to 2010. "It was neighbor helping neighbor and that was no surprise to those who lived here. To those outside the city, our citizens' responses to Harvey, Ike, Allison and Katrina showed the true character of the people who live here."

Shad Bogany of Better Homes and Gardens Real Estate Gary Greene assessed the situation similarly. "What I love about this city is that the people are so incredibly strong," said Bogany, who served as chair of the Houston Association of Realtors in 2002. "That's because I believe Houston is a state of mind, not just a place. The Harvey difference was people from all over the state and the country came to assist. The opposite occurred in New

Orleans when they had Katrina. It wasn't the same. Houston is the home of the oil wildcatters, who took risks and chances, and it's in our spirit to overcome challenges."

Houston leaders demonstrate a new sense of urgency. Being cloaked with a reputation for flooding can choke off growth and discourage would-be newcomers and corporate relocations.

Environmentalists believe new development west of Houston is a culprit. As more homes, streets, and parking lots are built, drainage is impacted in the city. Every day more concrete is poured in the flat Katy Prairie west of Houston, causing the disappearing grasslands to lose more of their ability to be a sponge for rainwater. Solutions need to arrive soon or the economy will suffer and homeowners could become flood victims again.

"We're at a crossroads for the future of Houston economically — that is where I see biggest challenges and opportunities, trying to rethink our approach to flooding," explains Jim Blackburn, professor, environmental law, Department of Civil and Environmental Engineering at Rice University and co-director, Severe Storm Prediction, Education and Evacuation from Disaster (SSPEED) Center.

"Flood control isn't the right term. Flood management is. Here in Houston, we will have to learn to live with water and learn to integrate water into our future. We need to incorporate water into the infrastructure of the city and county. We are not going to 'control' the Hurricane Harveys and Tropical Storm Allisons of the future. We have to understand how to manage that water. We have put down a lot of concrete that, over time, has increased flooding. Secondly, rainfall patterns are changing; they are becoming more intense and will get more intense in the future. Before all the concrete, the Katy Prairie held a lot of water naturally, but now it dumps a great deal of water into the bayous. We need to raise the money to buy out all the houses that are affected and cannot otherwise be protected and dedicate this land to hold and manage the water."

— JIM BLACKBURN, PROFESSOR OF
ENVIRONMENTAL LAW, RICE UNIVERSITY

THE STORM

Residents are heeding the call. Voters in Harris County passed a $2.5 billion bond measure in August 2018 to overhaul the region's flood-protection system, a year after Hurricane Harvey battered the Bayou City. The funds include $919 million for channel improvements, $386 million for detention basins, $220 million for floodplain land acquisition, $12.5 million for new floodplain mapping, and $1.25 million for an improved early flood warning system. Time will tell whether the spending plan can solve the problem.

"Texas' climate is changing. Most of the state has warmed between one-half and one degree Fahrenheit in the past century," says "What Climate Change Means for Texas," a report by the US Environmental Protection Agency. "Rainstorms are becoming more intense, and floods are becoming more severe. Along much of the coast, the sea is rising almost two inches per decade. In the coming decades, storms are likely to become more severe ..."

The severe storms are not the only threat hovering over the future of coastal Texas. Climate change is expected to bring rising sea levels, endangering the coastal properties eroding the beaches and destroying wetlands.

Studies and models for flood gates, seawalls and dikes continue to be discussed, although it will be years — or decades — before the proper solutions can be identified and constructed. Big storms will come again. Will Houston be prepared? Will any future storm be as big Hurricane Harvey?

Harvey started as a wave off the west coast of Africa in mid-August. It had escalated to a Category 4 storm by the time it slammed into Texas two weeks later. Harvey rapidly weakened and stalled over the area for four days, pouring down record rainfall over a very large area. The National Oceanic and Atmospheric Administration reported the highest storm total rainfall — 60.58 inches — was found in Nederland, a town east of Houston near Beaumont. Rainfall within a tenth of an inch of that total was recorded in Groves, a neighboring community. These both exceed the previous US rainfall record of fifty-two inches, set by Hurricane Hiki in Hawaii in 1950.

With rain rates outpacing the drainage capabilities in Houston, water levels in the bayous and streams rose abruptly overnight to record highs. Rivers and creek levels rose, inundating neighborhoods, washing out roads, and forcing residents to seek shelter on higher ground — or on the second floor of their home. Houston's flat landscape and hardpan clay do not absorb intense rainfall the way places with sandier soil do. And 50 inches of rain would swamp virtually any city in the world. With the city quickly filling with water, thousands of Houstonians had to be rescued from their homes.

Areas that were never flooded before received high water that inundated homes. Former Mayor White was sitting at his home in the upscale Memorial neighborhood of West Houston when the floodwaters came calling.

> "I was in the house when the water first came in," he recalls. "It was popping out of the electrical sockets! We built the house to withstand a 500-year event, but 50 inches of rain in four-and-a-half days was way off the charts and the releases from the dams caused a surge. There was water all over the house. We moved most of furniture upstairs, but we had to rebuild the first floor."

The city was simply not prepared for Harvey and is not ready for the storms in the future, says Blackburn.

> "We've got to figure out what we need to do to get ready for the storms we know are coming," he continues. "Basically, we need to clear dangerous areas of homes and dedicate the land to naturally retaining water — to flood management. There is a lot of natural land to the west of Houston, and we should make better use of them — maybe pay ranchers one hundred dollars an acre to restore the prairie for what it's good for. The Houston of the future must make room for the bayous and peel communities back from the bayous and add retention ponds and make larger channels. We need a future where Houston adapts to the changing forces of nature, and that's not where we are right now. If Houston continues to wallow in flooding, no one will want to come to the city. We need to be quite different in the twenty-first century than we were in the twentieth century."

Meyerland, an established community of some 2,300 homes on the city's southwest side, was particularly hard-hit during Harvey. Located near Brays Bayou — one of the primary ducts to carry stormwater to the Gulf of Mexico and drainage system for 127 square miles — Meyerland not only serves as the center of Jewish life in the city but also is one of Houston's most desirable neighborhoods. Congregation Beth Israel, which dates to the 1850s, has been at its Meyerland location across the street from the bayou for half a century. It never flooded before 2015 but has flooded three times in as many years. Several Jewish institutions, including the Evelyn Rubenstein Jewish Community Center and Seven Acres Jewish Senior Care, sustained heavy flood damage in the 2017 hurricane. On the southern bank of the bayou, the United Orthodox Synagogues, where people had walked to worship since 1961, was hit hard again and synagogue leaders decided to demolish the building a few months after Harvey's devastating blow.

"We did that to ourselves," says Blackburn. "Meyerland is the center of our Jewish community and it's culturally tied to particular pieces of real estate. But in the future, we're going to be hard pressed to protect Meyerland. Meyerland was protected by Brays Bayou and then the area upstream was developed. That increased the flow of water through areas like Meyerland. At the peak rainfall during Harvey, the flow was around 34,000 feet per second. Before the land was developed, it was only 8,000 feet per second. Maybe building levees for certain areas could protect the floodplain. Elevated homes are one solution, but that's going to get old — people keep evacuating, waiting for flooding to come back down. You may save your house, but you still will lose cars, and you'll have to muck out the garage. That is not a good way to live. Even with the Brays Bayou project completed, I do not see the flooding problems in that area solved anytime soon."

Amy Bernstein, who founded Bernstein Realty in 1985, points out the good news is that Meyerland is strong and residents are rebuilding.

"I feel Meyerland will be a desirable neighborhood again with a diverse mix of new construction, existing homes that have been elevated, and original homes that have been gutted and remodeled. The proximity of the Meyerland neighborhood remains ideal for many. There is also great confidence in the widening of the bayou project, with strong hope that it will minimize future flood occurrences."

— AMY BERNSTEIN, FOUNDER, BERNSTEIN REALTY

THE DAMS

Hurricane Harvey caused tremendous flooding, but so did the reservoirs designed to contain flood waters. The city has a history of flooding. After two massive floods, in 1929 and 1935, paralyzed the city, Houston sought solutions. The U.S. Army Corps of Engineers offered to build three reservoirs to contain the floodwaters of the future and protect the inner city. The Corps constructed Barker — which opened in 1945 — and Addicks three years later. The third dam to create the proposed White Oak Reservoir, was never constructed because the Corps did not have the funds. That shortcut to save money then proved to be a costly mistake for Houstonians decades later. As Houstonians searched for fixes after Harvey, building a third reservoir emerged as a possible solution — a solution that is backed by Mayor Turner. "But this time the Corps needs to keep such studies front and center, not on a shelf. I am confident that the Corps and Congress will move to build such a reservoir," Turner says.

Decades ago, the Corps purchased the land for its two reservoirs but did not buy the surrounding areas that could flood if the reservoirs ever filled to capacity — because it lacked the money. Throughout the ensuing years, real estate development continued in the area, with residential communities being built close to the edge of the reservoirs' backup zones. Many home buyers say they were never told they could face grave danger if a massive flood hit Houston and the water in the dams had to be released.

Then came Harvey. With so much rain over such a short period of time, the two reservoirs keeping Houston from experiencing catastrophic flooding were finally filled to capacity and could no longer contain the rising waters. The Corps said if it didn't begin releasing water, the volume of uncontrolled water around the dams would be higher and have a greater impact on the surrounding communities. No matter what they did, the excess water was coming one way or another.

"The flooding in Northwest Houston occurred not from rainfall but from the release of water from the reservoirs," says Dr. Jim Gaines, chief economist at the Real Estate Center at Texas A&M University.

> "They didn't give much warning, but even if they did, what were people going to do? They couldn't pick up their house and move it. The Army Corps of Engineers had never released that much water before and we hadn't seen that degree of flooding that occurred. But as I understand it, the Corps had no choice but to release water because there was going to be structural damage to the dam."
>
> — DR. JIM GAINES, TEXAS A&M UNIVERSITY

The result was homes in West Houston that had never flooded before were waist-deep in water. The neighborhoods didn't flood during Harvey — only afterward, when water was released from the near-to-capacity Addicks and Barker Reservoirs. Water released during the night quickly swamped downstream neighborhoods along Buffalo Bayou. Many homeowners didn't have flood insurance — why should they, since the area hadn't flooded before? The deluging of the Memorial and Energy Corridor neighborhoods southeast of the city's two main reservoirs, where nearly 200,000 Houstonians live, was unprecedented. Residents later complained that because of insufficient communication from the city and Harris County, they had no time to make decisions that would have allowed them to save their cars and other possessions.

HARVEY'S EFFECT ON REAL ESTATE

Houston's real estate world changed dramatically during those rain-soaked four days in August 2017. Harvey's waters — including those from the dams — inundated homes and displaced thousands of Houstonians. Some property owners remained under financial pressure more than a year after Harvey.

"I don't think we've seen the final impact yet," says Bogany. "We've seen change and devastation in neighborhoods around Houston, but we haven't seen the total impact because foreclosures have not hit the market yet. Some Houston areas [that] were a neighborhood of owners now will become a neighborhood of renters because their homes flooded so many times. You've got homes in those neighborhoods that may have flooded, and people don't want to live in the house. So, investors come in and buy the house and lease it."

Harvey caused numerous economic problems at the margins of the housing market because the supply of affordable homes in Houston constricted. "We've not fully recovered, particularly with all the property that was damaged, but the Houston economy is strong," said Mayor White.

Houston is a city of doers and not complainers, said White.

"Houston is a work in progress. Every generation has some opportunity and responsibility of taking Houston in a new direction. We have the highest concentration of engineers in the country, because of our legacy of leadership in the energy industry. We have a relatively low cost of living and a very deep, small-business community with a lot of entrepreneurs. It's my experience from being mayor that the vast majority of Houstonians view our diversity of background, cultures, and religions as our strengths. We have a diversified economy. Houston has a lot of service businesses outside energy – we have a very strong center of medical research and strong manufacturing employment compared to other areas of the US. We have a very strong future ahead of us."

— BILL WHITE, FORMER MAYOR

A year after Harvey, the Houston economy was kicking into high-gear again, with strong job growth and record-setting existing home activity that was more than 5 percent ahead of the pace in 2017.

"Houston has proven over fifty years to be a resilient, dynamic economic market. It is still the energy capital of the world and it can't be ignored," says Dr. Gaines of Texas A&M. "It's the spirit of Houstonians and the emergence as a major, strategic economic hub in the state and in the nation."

MOVING ON

While the flooding that occurred in the aftermath of Harvey was a shock to most, West Houston still remains an extremely desirable area, despite the close proximity to the reservoirs, said Realtor Bernstein. "Most people rebuilding in this neighborhood feel confident that this was a very rare incident and for many an opportunity to move into a neighborhood that was once price restrictive," continued Bernstein. "Many homes are being remodeled and rebuilt; the new construction homes will blend well with the homes that are being remodeled. These West Houston neighborhoods, in my opinion, will once again be extremely sought-after in the future."

Houstonians will rebuild — as they have before. Harvey's destruction came after two major flood events — the 2016 "Tax Day" flood (so named because it fell on the deadline to file federal income taxes). Eleven months before that residents endured the 2015 Memorial Day flood that also crippled the city. Together, the floods killed 16 people and inflicted well over $1 billion in damage.

Bernstein's own home flooded on Memorial Day in 2015 and Tax Day in 2016, but it did not flood during Harvey. "From those experiences, I learned that when that much rain comes down in a short period of time some streets in Houston are just flood prone," she continues.

> "Because I love my neighborhood and my home, I have learned to keep materials to lift my furniture, rugs and anything else off of the ground handy if it appears that the water will approach my home. I also learned that although it is a terrible experience to live through a flood and the experience takes an extreme emotional toll on a person, the devastating experience is something that can be repaired. And often becomes better than it was before."
>
> — AMY BERNSTEIN

In April 2016, a storm system dumped more than a foot of rain on the Houston area, resulting in catastrophic flooding. From April 17-18, an average of 12 inches-16 inches of rain fell on the region in the span of twelve hours, flooding neighborhoods from Katy to Meyerland to Greenspoint. At one point, the rainfall rates reached an estimated 4 inches per hour. Greenspoint was one of the hardest-hit areas, where hundreds of families had to be rescued from their homes.

Eight to ten inches were recorded in the northwest and southwest areas of the city during the 2015 Memorial Day flood, with the heaviest accumulation — 11 inches — at Brays Bayou and Beltway 8. Some 952 homes were substantially damaged and more than five thousand properties were impacted citywide in 2015.

The recent storms — Tax Day, Memorial Day, and Hurricane Harvey — showed a different image of Houston to the world — that Houston and Harris County were flood prone. "That image can harm us if we don't fix it," said Harris County Judge Ed Emmett.

"Weather conditions and development paths are changing. That's why we're having so much flooding. Meyerland didn't used to flood; 610 didn't used to go under water. That's the challenge – fixing the problem. The county can do its part, but the city and state have to do their part, too. We've never focused on solving our flooding problem; it has never been the priority in the past. But after these three major storms, it has to be the priority. If we don't get that straight, the rest doesn't matter."

Houstonians are confident they will get it right this time. They have the resiliency and fortitude to do it because they've done it before. "Perhaps it's because we grew up as an independent nation. We've learned to take care of ourselves," said Emmett. "I also think it's the ranching and farming mentality that built Texas — you did the work and you survived, and if you didn't do the work, you didn't survive. People helped each other."

With Harvey, Houston experienced a climate-induced storm long before other cities will have to deal with the problem, said Blackburn.

"We have to envision living with water," he continued. "We are not going to control the floods of the future. We are going to have to live with them and manage them. Water is a citizen of Houston and needs its own property. From a real estate perspective, there is a new client in town called 'water.' In the past, we tried to almost deal with it as an afterthought, to push it away. That doesn't work. That was an engineering approach and only engineering is not sufficient. We need to bring nature back into the mix and have to do more planning than we have in the past. We need to develop a different type of city — one that can live with water."

In the short-term, Houston has been moving quickly to get ready for the next one. "We have already learned how to do things better in dealing with epic flooding; we have acquired more rescue boats, as one example," Mayor Turner says. "Hurricanes have come and gone since Houston started. But now the heavy rains seem to come more often. While we work for long-term lessening of man-made climate change, we must be better adapters in the short term."

Hurricane Harvey won't be enough to stunt the city's future growth. The flooding problem will be fixed, Turner says, and in the decades ahead Houston will pass Chicago to become the third largest city in the nation.

"Houston will continue to dynamically transform itself again and again, adapting faster and better than its competitors as it takes its place as the nation's third most populous city," Mayor Turner says when asked about the decades ahead. "Market forces and government will work together to make the city more resilient."

There is no guarantee, of course, that solutions will arrive in Bayou City.

Houston's growth challenges — flooding and drainage, transit and traffic — are significant and fixing them will be costly and difficult for elected leaders and government officials. Houston's private sector has its own share of problems, but none more pronounced than the cloud hanging over Houston's office market: some fifty million square feet of office space — equivalent to fifty downtown towers — was vacant as 2018 came to a close, according to NAI Partners. And as Houston's skyscraper owners know, fifty million square feet of vacancy does not disappear overnight.

4
DOWNTOWN SKYSCRAPERS AND THEIR STRUGGLE TO REMAIN RELEVANT

HOUSTON'S SKYLINE is not a finished work. New towers continue to rise in downtown. But the new breed of buildings have unusual traits — rooftop gardens, balcony-like "sky atrium" gathering places, and lobbies with a hotel feel.

The new towers embrace today's skyscraper battlecry: "more amenities." The new office buildings are viewed as recruitment tools that can seduce and retain millennial employees for the tower's tenants. Windowless workspaces and cramped cubicles are out. Collaborative spaces without assigned desks are in. More glass, more windows, and better views are worth paying for, from the tenant's perspective, if the company's offices translate into having a stronger roster of employees. Houston is the natural place for new trends in office space to be introduced because the city's downtown was instrumental in breaking the glass-box trends that once ruled architectural circles. Houston — the wildcatters town — was the place for discarding the norms.

Rewind forty years to consider the twin skyscrapers that turned things upside down in the early seventies. The two 36-story trapezoidal towers of dark glass, positioned next to a 115-foot-high glassed-in courtyard, are among the most widely recognized skyscrapers in the world. When the twin-tower development was completed, the jaw-dropping edifices — pop artist Andy Warhol came to Houston to capture the image in Polaroid photos – launched a new era of corporate headquarters. The structure also catapulted a former air conditioning salesman to international design and real estate fame and initiated the postmodern period in American architecture.

The development was Pennzoil Place, the twin-towered complex created by architects Philip Johnson and John Burgee. Triangular lobbies are covered with glass to create a greenhouse feel. The top seven floors of each tower were crafted as part of a remarkable slanted roof. This unusual, dark-skinned skyscraper, Pennzoil Place — completed in 1975 — was named the "Building of the Decade" by noted New York Times architecture critic Ada Louise Huxtable and gained prominence in the architectural world for shattering the modernist glass box made popular by the disciples of Ludwig Mies van der Rohe.

Equally important, Pennzoil Place was the creation of a then little-known real estate entrepreneur who had begun his real career as a builder of warehouses and low-rise office buildings on Houston's Richmond Avenue but who was driven to step onto a global stage and change skylines with noteworthy towers by prominent architects around the world. He was Gerald D. Hines, and the Houston-based firm he founded, now called simply Hines, has grown to become one of the world's largest privately owned real estate investment, development, and management firms. Today it has a presence in more than two hundred cities in two dozen countries and boasts a portfolio with more than $100 billion of assets under management. And Pennzoil Place still makes a statement in downtown Houston.

"Pennzoil Place was a breakthrough," says Stephen Fox, architectural historian and a lecturer at the Rice School of Architecture and the Gerald D. Hines College of Architecture at the University of Houston. Fox, author of the AIA Houston Architectural Guide (2012), has studied Houston for decades.

"It elevated Gerald Hines to the status of a patron of architecture and boosted Philip Johnson's career. With Pennzoil, he established a new paradigm for high-rise architecture that proved to be prophetic. Pennzoil Place created a new architectural standard. The quest for sculptural design in skyscrapers that Pennzoil Place began prevails today: to build sculpturally configured structures that become instant landmarks and icons. Subsequent downtown buildings sought to rise to its level of quality. Forty years later, Pennzoil Place is still an extraordinary presence."

— STEPHEN FOX, ARCHITECTURAL HISTORIAN, LECTURER AT RICE SCHOOL OF ARCHITECTURE AND THE GERALD D. HINES COLLEGE OF ARCHITECTURE AT THE UNIVERSITY OF HOUSTON.

Pennzoil Place put Houston on the map as a city on the rise, a metropolis where everything was possible. With the escalating of oil prices in the 1970s, Houston — already the energy capital of the country — grew exponentially. Brash and bigger was the Houston mantra. Hell bent on one-upping other cities, the city's amped-up entrepreneurs — especially real estate developers — were convinced that the sky was the limit. Until it wasn't, and the sky fell down.

Oil prices plummeted from around $35 a barrel to less than $10 because of an oil glut caused by shrinking demand following the 1970s energy crisis. The Houston economy, more diversified in recent decades, but always susceptible to vicious free-falls in oil prices, suffered significantly in the 1980s. Houston was dealt a tough hand, a triple whammy, actually — the collapse of the savings and loan industry combined with falling oil prices and an unprecedented wave of property foreclosures. The Texas economy was crushed in the mid-1980s.

Around 1980, an oversupply of oil had developed, resulting in a six-year decline in the price of crude. In late 1985, there were nearly 2,300 rigs drilling wells operating in the US. A year later, there were barely a thousand. Accordingly, Houston's real estate industry screeched to a halt. The ups and downs of the city's real estate markets marched in step with the oil business. Big, bold, and brash were followed by failure and foreclosure. That was the Houston pattern — boom and bust — but always recovering.

Real estate runs deep — on the chromosomal level — in Houston. The town was founded on selling real estate — and it became an entrepreneurial mecca almost from the moment it was founded — a year after Texas gained its independence from Mexico. In August 1836, two New York promoters — John Allen and his bookkeeper brother Augustus — acquired 6,642 acres of raw land for $1.50 an acre around the banks of Buffalo Bayou. The brothers hyped the property, naming the city after the hero of the revolution, Sam Houston, a Texian general in the war against Mexico. The town of Houston was the capital of the Republic of Texas and soon its population boomed into the hundreds. But promotion, optimism, and boosterism can only conceal so much before reality emerges: Houston was built on a swamp and mosquitos thrived. Hundreds of residents in the new town died from yellow fever. That prompted the relocation of the Republic of Texas' capital to Austin in 1839, marking the first real setback for Houston's growth.

Decades later, Houston locked into another growth spurt, becoming the financial capital for the fast-growing petroleum industry following the discovery of oil at the Spindletop oil field in southeast Texas in 1901. The city's race to expansion continued almost unabated throughout the twentieth century. The Port of Houston boomed. The Texas Medical Center was born. With the annexation of surrounding territory and new suburbs, Houston expanded its economic base. And in the early

1960s, NASA's Manned Spacecraft Center was built on the southeast side.

"Historically, Houston followed the same development patterns of other Southwestern and Texan cities," says Fox. "This has to do with the time it developed and the technology of the nineteenth and twentieth centuries. First came the railroad, then the streetcar, and finally the automobile. By the mid-point of the twentieth century, Houston experienced the development of metropolitan suburban sprawl."

Downtown Houston had solidified around the oil companies located there to be close to their bankers, law firms, and other service companies. Enter the son of a Gary, Indiana, steelworker who came to Houston in 1948 with no money, but plenty of ambition. Gerald D. Hines took a room at the YMCA and exercised his determination to succeed. The Purdue University-educated engineer signed on with an air-conditioning and ventilation company but before long, he started making real estate deals, gaining experience that would enable him to transform Houston's cityscape.

"Hines has left an indelible mark on the Houston skyline," adds Michael Anderson, executive vice president of Houston-based Colvill Office Properties.

"Pennzoil Place is still one of the more recognizable buildings in downtown, and a beautiful piece of architecture. Hines' passion for quality is unmatched, and Hines continues to be a leader in high-performance building design. Hines' recent announcement that they will move their global headquarters to downtown is exciting news and fitting for them to be in a location where they have had such a huge impact on the built environment."

— MICHAEL ANDERSON, EXECUTIVE VICE PRESIDENT COLVILL OFFICE PROPERTIES.

For more than a half-century, Hines has added pieces to the Houston skyline. The Hines era downtown began in the 1960s with Shell Oil, the U.S. subsidiary of Royal Dutch Shell and one of the so-called Seven Sisters — the seven largest oil companies in the world. At Shell's headquarters in New York, executives were looking to cut costs, and the high price of office space was an obvious money-saving solution waiting to be tapped.

It would eventually require a monumental decision by Shell leadership: Agree to relocate the firm's operating and corporate headquarters from Manhattan to Houston. Although he had never developed a building of this magnitude, Gerald Hines convinced Shell he could develop an office tower that would be more energy efficient and be more affordable. Hines retained the services of Chicago architects from Skidmore, Owings & Merrill firm for design. With an exterior of white, Italian Travertine marble, the One Shell Plaza was soon the talk of Houston. Completed in 1971, the million square-foot structure reigned as the tallest tower in Texas for years, although these days One Shell Plaza is just a portion of Houston's over-achieving skyline — and Shell Oil has vacated the premises that bore its name, moving to a corporate campus in West Houston and abandoning downtown.

Corporations were wooed by a series of new Hines towers that followed.

After Pennzoil Place, Hines created Houston's tallest building, a 75-story, 1.7 million-square-foot office tower clad in pale gray polished granite. Completed in 1982, the development includes a public granite-paved pedestrian plaza with a sculpture by Joan Miró, "Personage and Birds" — the largest Miró sculpture ever commissioned. The building was first known as Texas Commerce Tower, the local bank that occupied at first, and later as JPMorgan Chase Tower. Over the years, the bank has eliminated its office space in the building, and it closed its branch bank there in late 2018. The tower is now named after its address, 600 Travis, bank spokesman Greg Hassell says.

After the Chase Tower, Hines reunited with Philip Johnson and John Burgee for the Bank of America Center, a 56-story tower near the Theater District. Completed in 1983, the neo-Gothic building is clad in Napoleon red granite. Originally wrapped inside the historic building is the former Western Union building, which was hidden by a granite facade. It has been unseen by the public for decades. However, thanks to a new $20 million effort, the "long-dormant" Western Union space is being brought out into the open as a restaurant topped by a floor of a new office space that adds thirty thousand square feet to the skyscraper, now in the hands of M-M Properties.

Hines is responsible for a number of other buildings in downtown including: the 55-story 1100 Louisiana building; the 48-story 609 Main at Texas, which opened in early 2017; and the new 32-story Aris Market Square, a multifamily tower designed by Ziegler Cooper Architects.

What lies ahead for downtown Houston is again being dictated by Hines. In 2018, Hines and Canada's Ivanhoé Cambridge began construction on an innovative project that will house Hines' new global headquarters, a major law firm and other tenants. The building will be located on Texas Avenue at the former site of the Houston Chronicle. (In 2016, the newspaper relocated to the former Houston Post property along the Southwest Freeway near Loop 610.) Hines' new 47-story skyscraper, designed by Pelli Clarke Pelli Architects, will have the earmarks of new thinking in designing buildings for today's tenants. The one million square-foot tower will have a hotel-like lobby, multiple restaurant and beverage outlets, more networking spaces, and public gardens on level twelve. The structure represents a building design aimed to support employee recruiting, retention, and collaboration among the office workers, in line with new trends.

"All of these [new] buildings provide what many companies are looking for in today's work environment: a lot of natural light, energy efficiency, and amenities," says Tim Relyea, executive vice chairman of Cushman & Wakefield of Texas.

> "Both 609 Main and the new building on the former Chronicle site have 10-foot floor-to-ceiling windows and under-floor HVAC systems and many other base building design features such as core through restrooms, oversized freight elevators, wider fire stairwells, and in the case of the Chronicle site, three fire stairwells to accommodate the new code requirements. These new buildings also have stellar amenities such as conference centers, fitness centers, and new dining options."
>
> — TIM RELYEA, EXECUTIVE VICE CHAIRMAN OF CUSHMAN & WAKEFIELD, TEXAS.

Unlike skyscrapers from the prior generation, the newest Hines tower starts without an oil company in-tow. It's anchored by the Vinson & Elkins law firm. This reflects the rewriting of downtown's tenant roster in recent years.

Numerous energy companies still have offices in downtown Houston, but a number of big oil and gas corporations have departed. "Most of the historic downtown energy companies —

Exxon Mobil, Shell, Devon, Texaco, Conoco, Burlington — have moved out or been acquired, disappearing" from the central business district, explains Sanford W. Criner, CBRE vice chairman and native Houstonian.

> "Traditionally, the big oil companies were downtown along with the big banks and large law firms associated with them. That was when business for such global firms was still, in many ways, local. Humble Oil was from this era, before it became Exxon and then Exxon Mobil. Executive functions, as well as related legal and finance work was done downtown. Now, energy companies no longer need the local web of legal and finance support on which they depended, and their locational drivers are more likely to be based around their engineers who want to be in the suburbs close to their homes."
>
> — SANFORD W. CRINER, VICE CHAIRMAN
> CBRE, HOUSTON

Until the 1970s, he adds, there was very little office development in the suburbs. That's changed and so has downtown. "Different types of companies now — law and professional firms and banks — are willing to pay higher rates to be downtown in high-quality buildings," says Criner. "They do that because they want quality of place that only downtown can provide. Downtown activities have been getting better for a long time and will continue to do so."

Downtown's emergence as a better place to live comes as the many people in the millennial generation have the desire for a walkable environment with lifestyle and entertainment options. Being able to walk to work — or ride a bike — is attractive to millennials, as is taking light-rail transit. Driving alone in a car on a crowded freeway for a long commute is not popular with anyone. If recruitment and retention of urban-minded millennials is a priority, it raises questions about the development of corporate campuses in far-flung suburbs. Will the next generation prefer to work in downtown buildings a few blocks from their apartment or in the suburban corporate fortress reachable only by freeway? Maybe the millennial generation, which has been slow to embrace home buying, will warm up to the concept of the suburban campus workplace when they seek to buy homes in affordable suburbs. Meanwhile, despite the desire to recruit an urban-oriented millennial workforce, downtown's 45-story building at 800 Bell was vacated in 2015 by Exxon Mobil when it moved to its new corporate campus north of Houston. The downtown building has remained vacant for years. Some say Exxon Mobil's creation of the massive suburban campus signifies that the company bowed to the desires of the firm's influential executives and older engineers, while demoting the tastes of urban-oriented millennials.

Downtown Houston's most recent office vacancy outbreak began when oil prices began to fall in 2014, as a worldwide oversupply developed. At a fateful meeting in Vienna on Thanksgiving Day 2014, OPEC voted to decline to make production cuts. The move resulted in a bloodbath in the energy industry. A rapid descent from more than $100 a barrel to less than $30, created layoffs and significant office vacancy in Houston. Energy companies — the backbone of Houston office tenancy for almost a century — are not expanding. Many are shrinking. Even as oil prices recover, it has become apparent that oil companies will not be an instant savior to absorb the office oversupply.

"Although the price of oil is steadily increasing, I see a mindset change in this tenant group and expect it to be very cautious for the foreseeable future," says Charles Herder, principal shareholder and co-chairman of Colliers International in Houston.

Nothing on the horizon suggests that energy firms will move from an era of caution into an expansion mode. So the Houston office market claws ahead, trying to make progress in filling the 50 million square feet of vacant space around the city as 2018 ended. The city suffered further embarrassment by failing to make the Amazon HQ2 short list of twenty finalist cities. Amazon had stipulated a massive office space requirement of eight million square feet. After the Amazon strikeout, the city responded by initiating an effort to create an innovation technology district with a business incubator and an academic presence, but that growth will take years to mature. No quick fix will arise through economic development efforts to fill the empty buildings. The office market recovery will require basic blocking and tackling and more time — plus stabilization and a resumption of hiring in the energy industry.

Even with office vacancy looming large, more new office space has risen on the downtown skyline, such as Skanska USA's 35-story office tower on a block bounded by Capitol, Rusk, Milam, and Travis streets. Designed by Gensler, the tower, slated to be complete in the first half of 2019, will have 754,000 square feet of office space with more than 30,000 square feet of retail and restaurant space. The tunnel level will include a culinary market designed by architect Michael Hsu. The Skanska tower will be anchored by Bank of America, which will vacate a classic Hines tower nearby to occupy 210,000 square feet in the new Skanska building.

As for the building that started it all for Hines, One Shell Plaza has been renovated and more than half of the 800,000 square feet of vacant space Shell left behind has been re-leased. Hines was retained as redeveloper of the companion building, the 26-story Two Shell Plaza, renamed as 811 Louisiana, a 578,000-square-foot tower in the center of downtown. Two lessons can be extracted from One and Two Shell Plazas: (1) significant redevelopment is required for office buildings to remain relevant in the marketplace, and (2) even vacant holes as big as Shell's can be backfilled, eventually.

"Shell Oil did not relocate because they were unhappy with downtown. The move was a real estate decision based on having excess space in their 'owned' facility/campus in West Houston compared to their leased premises in downtown," says Relyea of Cushman & Wakefield.

"The oil and gas downturn in 2014 caught Shell Oil, like many other energy companies, with substantially more real estate than needed and they made a business decision based on their operations and not solely locational preferences. Fortunately, the majority of the vacated Shell Oil space has been subleased, so the relocation was not as painful to the market as originally anticipated."

Downtown Houston, frequently called the Central Business District, is evolving again into more than a business location. Once stereotyped as a place where tumbleweeds blew down the streets on weekends, downtown Houston has been revived. Over the past two decades, more than $9 billion in public and private investments have been made toward achieving a vision of a dynamic and vibrant place to live, work, and play. Multifamily developers received a $15,000 tax break for each apartment unit constructed in the downtown from 2012 to 2016, thanks to the city's Downtown Living Initiative. Downtown now has more than 8,000 residents, a sizable increase from 3,800 residents when the Downtown Living tax break program was started.

> "Downtown is picking up traction because it's establishing itself as a place to live. We've had residential downtown for years, of course, but not much. Downtown was not a player in the multifamily market except for places like The Rice," says Bob Eury, president of the nonprofit Central Houston Inc., a downtown planning organization. "We'd like to have thirty thousand residences downtown over the next two decades. In looking at other major cities, when you hit twenty thousand to thirty thousand residents, you have enough population so it is a market to itself. You can have grocery and retail there. We are starting to pick that up today as we move toward that goal."

Houston's light rail, along with other public transit, now connects the central business district to the major employment center of Texas Medical Center, the Museum District, and several universities. Developers respond with mid-rise and high-rise multifamily apartments located along the transit line.

The trend in Houston nowadays, mirroring a national direction, is a revitalization of downtown into an environment that is walkable and appealing. The bridge to this end has been the noncommercial components that have been added over the last twenty years, including Minute Maid Park, Discovery Green, and Toyota Center — places that add to downtown's appeal. "They had nothing to do with office buildings, but they were important in creating the place where people — and, increasingly, corporations — want to be," says CBRE's Criner. "A huge amount of residential has been built downtown and the result is a more robust downtown environment."

The downtown environment has been enhanced with more hotels, including the 328-room JW Marriott Houston Downtown, an adaptive reuse of a century-old building on Main Street. Midway Cos., in partnership with the Valencia Group, also chimed-in with the new 223-room Hotel Alessandra, which is part of Midway's GreenStreet, a 570,000-square-foot, mixed-use development on three blocks along Dallas Street.

Over the last ten years, there have been many more new additions of residential, restaurants, and hotels in downtown. But one new development carries with it hope for expanding into a new generation: the Kinder High School for the Performing and Visual Arts. The $88 million school sits on a block bounded by Austin, Caroline, Capitol, and Rusk streets. Most of the students will be whisked away to the suburbs at the end of the day. But maybe a few of the families involved at the school will consider living in downtown.

Maybe some attainable housing solutions will arise in downtown for families. It's probably impossible, even though the borders of downtown proper are being erased. The planned removal of downtown's Pierce Elevated freeway, which has served as a Berlin Wall discouraging downtown growth from moving into Midtown, adds a hopeful note to southern downtown and the surrounding area. Maybe downtown is a place where only young professionals and empty nesters will reside — that is the conventional wisdom. But great strides have been made in revitalizing downtown Houston in the last decade and an abundance of newness will emerge in the decade ahead. Doubters should proceed with caution.

5

THE GRAND PARKWAY: AMERICA'S LONGEST LOOP

It is one of those unbelievable schemes that have marked Houston's history — an ambitious, mind-boggling undertaking that is one of the most ambitious and massive highway construction projects ever in Texas — or the nation. Upon completion, it will be the largest highway loop in the nation, according to the Texas highway agency. After almost six decades of planning, development, and construction, and billions of dollars, Houston's plan to build a massive freeway ring spanning seven counties is about halfway built.

The new highway lured the nation's largest oil company, which built a three million square-foot campus. Then came the Daikin air conditioner factory, which has thousands of employees working in a four million square-foot building, the largest tilt-wall building ever built in the world, according to the Tilt-Up Concrete Association.

With a powerful magnetism, the highway has attracted billions in new development — new housing, retail centers, office buildings, and warehouses. Nothing transforms open prairie like new roads. Dozens of miles of this new road will be built in the coming years, transporting growth to the suburbs and exurbs. It will be the spine of expansion for years to come.

Proponents say it will provide access to affordable land for home building and development, in addition to vast transportation benefits. Critics say the roadway leads to sprawl and exacerbates flooding for the region.

First proposed in the 1960s, the roadway — formally known as Texas 99 but more commonly referred to as the Grand Parkway — is its own wonder — large enough to circumscribe the whole state of Rhode Island.

Expected to be finished before the end of 2022, the Grand Parkway will circumvent the Greater Houston area. The 184-mile loop will connect the farthest outskirts of the Houston area and the third roadway loop within the Houston-Woodlands-Sugar Land metropolitan area.

The concept behind the massive Grand Parkway project was that the nearly 200-mile roadway would help alleviate future highway congestion and spur growth and development as the Bayou City expanded. A loop of such magnitude had been needed on Houston's north side for years, said proponents, who also predicted that — once completed — it would help ease traffic flows on Houston's already overwhelmed freeway arteries, including the notorious Highway 290.

The Grand Parkway, they added, would be what Loop 610 (completed in the 1970s) and Beltway 8 (completed in the 1980s) used to be.

Divided into eleven sectors for construction and funding purposes, and after years of work about half of the Grand Parkway loop was built and open to traffic by early 2019. The first section was opened in Fort Bend County in 1994 and almost immediately the land rush was on. The multi-billion-dollar Texas Department of Transportation roadway has fueled job creation as well as new homes, offices, mixed-use projects, apartments, warehouses, hospitals, and other development in previously inaccessible land across Northwest Houston.

"Its importance and impact on Houston real estate cannot be overstated," says veteran Houston land broker Stan Creech. "It has opened thousands of acres for land development to accommodate Houston's inevitable growth."

The Grand Parkway represents more than an opportunity to build homes and stores and schools: It also represents the expansion away from central urban areas into low-density and car-dependent communities. "The Grand Parkway continues the same suburban sprawl pattern of low density development as its predecessors, Loop 610 and the West Belt," says Scott Ziegler, senior principal at Houston-based Ziegler Cooper Architects.

> "Suburban sprawl has not been kind to Houston as it continues to hamper our mobility by making our freeway more congested and diminishing our quality of life. We are also experiencing skyrocketing fuel costs, increased environmental pollution, and our forests are being paved with concrete to build new roads and subdivisions, which leave our entire city more vulnerable to future flooding like Hurricane Harvey."
>
> — SCOTT ZIEGLER, SENIOR PRINCIPAL
> ZIEGLER COOPER ARCHITECTS.

Many voices articulate the charge that Houston's third loop is exacerbating flooding in the region. Thousands of acres of Houston-area prairie have been converted to new development. And without the sponge of the prairie, rainfall can create problems.

CONFRONTING HOUSTON'S BIGGEST CHALLENGE

Equally important, low-density development facilitated by Grand Parkway continues to burden Houston's ability to financially sustain the high infrastructure cost of roads, utilities, and public services for police and fire protection, Ziegler continues. "I believe Houston's biggest challenge for the twenty-first century will be undoing the damage resulting from suburban sprawl and transitioning to a more sustainable high density urban growth model for our future," Ziegler adds.

> "Houston is currently in the very early stages of urbanization and densification and it is more important, now than ever before, to plan appropriately for our future growth. Millennials are attracted to the twenty-four/seven urban lifestyle and empty nesters are cashing out from their low-debt homes and leasing luxury apartments in urban areas, so they can attend cultural events, performing arts, sporting events, and dine out at all the new foodie restaurant options."
>
> — SCOTT ZIEGLER

In Houston, where bigger is usually defined as better, Ziegler is in the minority. While some would refer to it as "sprawl," most real estate people consider the Grand Parkway-enabled development as "expansion."

> "Growth is a good thing," says Ted Nelson, president and chief operating officer of Newland Communities — one of the nation's largest developers of planned communities — "and if done properly it is a *great* thing. A key component of good growth is planning for and building the infrastructure needed to support growth. From a traffic planning point of view, loop roadway systems are a critical piece of transportation infrastructure. I want Houston to continue to be able to accommodate growth and I truly hope that I never live to see the day that Houston becomes a Detroit as there are no winners when cities cease growing and begin to contract."

The Grand Parkway directs future growth and has the power to move mountains, even when the mountain is the nation's largest energy company.

It is widely cited as one of the reasons global energy giant Exxon Mobil Corp. chose a 385-acre site to build a corporate campus near where the Grand Parkway and Interstate 45 intersect north of the Houston city limits. In 2014, Exxon Mobil opened that twenty-building, three million-square-foot corporate campus where some ten thousand employees work. The Grand Parkway is doing more than simply funneling Exxon Mobil employees to work. Significant growth – additional office, hotel, and multifamily projects — have been built adjacent to Exxon Mobil.

As the Grand Parkway opens up vast swaths of suburban land, it brings considerable population growth and opportunity.

Property values along the Grand Parkway have skyrocketed since the first section opened two and a half decades ago. Land fronting on the Grand Parkway offers the best visibility and accessibility, says land broker Creech. Prices for land fronting the Grand Parkway have increased multifold. "An example is ninety acres we sold on the Grand Parkway and Kingsland to an investor for $40,000 per acre and resold for $225,000 per acre," says Creech. "The continuously expanding Houston population makes the Grand Parkway a transportation necessity." It's a road that leads to the "American Dream," which is defined by Creech as "owning a home in a great neighborhood with good schools, churches, and lifestyle amenities."

The American Dream is translated into something else in Houston: Master Planned Communities (MPCs). MPCs are very large scale; the number and variety of amenities clearly separates this breed from a normal plan for a housing subdivision. As newcomers arrived in Houston's no-zoning environment, the MPCs offer the certainty of a planning framework of the future.

"And they grew into prominence in Houston because of a need. The ancient Greek philosopher Plato reportedly said, 'Necessity is the mother of invention.' And that's true in Houston," said David Jarvis, senior vice presidentat John Burns Real Estate Consulting.

"Houston is well known as the largest city in America without zoning. Some people have described the city as one giant unmade bed. As a resident here, you would go to the suburbs usually to buy a house and move into a master planned community. There have been some awesome MPCs that have had good shepherds like the late energy entrepreneur George Mitchell who started The Woodlands. Mitchell — who is known as the father of fracking — envisioned what those 28,000 acres north of Houston could become. The Woodlands is one of many examples of awesome MPCs in the area that included schools and retail and residences – what you get in a lot of cities around the US but that maybe we didn't get enough of in Houston MPCs became a tremendous part of the Houston landscape. At one time, MPCs commanded 50 percent of all home sales in the city. Now 30-35 percent of the all the homes sold in Houston are in MPCs. I don't think any other city could say that."

— DAVID JARVIS, SENIOR VICE PRESIDENT, JOHN BURNS REAL ESTATE CONSULTING.

Jarvis says MPCs in Houston will continue to have a big future. "Millennials are growing up, paying down student debt, and thinking about where they want to live when they get married and have children," he explained. "So where do they want to live? The suburbs."

Over the past half-century, developers have carved out scores of master planned communities in Houston that provide places for families to sleep, play, learn, and sometimes work in close proximity. Unlike other parts of the country dotted with mountains, valleys, and forests, Houston is planted on flat coastal prairie. Passersby looked at the land and saw nondescript grassland. Real estate entrepreneurs looked beyond the flatness and saw opportunity. No matter how long the daily commute would be, people working in Houston needed reasonably priced square footage for their families in a planned community with good schools. So the developers staked claims to suburban and exurban tracts and began perfecting the MPC genre with projects of one thousand acres or more.

Over time, Houston became the king of the master planned community thanks to an abundance of inexpensive land open for development and the convenient way developers were able to create municipal utility districts (MUDs) to provide water and sewer services fairly easily, floating bonds to finance it all.

THE HIT PARADE OF MASTER PLANNED COMMUNITIES

Starting to work in the 1960s, Friendswood Development, formerly a subsidiary of Humble Oil, created Clear Lake City and Kingwood. George Mitchell was getting national attention with The Woodlands. And Hines Interests developed First Colony, a 10,000-acre community in Fort Bend County on the southwest side. These pioneering projects set the stage for the emergence of a new generation of MPCs supported by the Grand Parkway.

No place was changed by the Grand Parkway like Cinco Ranch.

Cinco Ranch is about twenty-five miles west of downtown Houston and ten miles north of the Fort Bend County seat of Richmond. It began thirty-five years ago with one of the largest raw land transactions in the history of Houston. Cinco Ranch Venture — U.S. Home, the Mischer Corporation, and American General Corporation — purchased 5,000 acres of the Cinco Ranch, a working ranch that was destined to become a master planned development. The price: $84 million. The year: 1984.

When the ranch was sold to the developers, nobody knew the savings and loan crisis (which would eventually result in the failure of more than a thousand financial institutions) was just around the corner. The S&L problem, combined with the impact of the 1980s energy downturn (a barrel of oil sank to below $10) and Houston was trapped in a vicious economy crash that stalled the start of Cinco Ranch's development for years. After the economy stabilized, the community's first homes were finally sold in 1991.

Then, the early 1990s delivered a high-octane accelerant for Cinco Ranch home sales – the opening of the Grand Parkway.

"The connection between IH-10 West and FM 1093 [Westheimer] through Cinco Ranch area was the first segment constructed and an important element in the growth of the greater Katy area," says developer Ted Nelson of Newland Communities.

Nelson was a key member of the team that was instrumental in planning and developing Cinco Ranch — later helping to build other Houston-area master planned communities, including Telfair, Seven Meadows, Greatwood and Summerwood.

The initial segment of the Grand Parkway did more than lead traffic to Cinco Ranch. It opened up the western side of Houston. "I believe that the segment that connects IH-69 South to IH-69 North (US 59) is the most important segment, as it provides a significant alternative for southbound traffic on IH-45 and IH-69 that previously had to come into and through the city to be able to continue their journey whether to the west or south without traveling through the city," Nelson says.

If the Grand Parkway hadn't been built, Nelson adds, Houston would have more congestion and growth would have to be accommodated even farther out on the spokes — farther out IH-10, IH-45, IH-69. Most of the US cities that developed "post automobile" are very similar in terms of density and that means a density of residential that is typically between two thousand and three thousand people per square mile. "Were the neighborhoods inside Loop 610 any different in terms of density when they were built substantially different than the density of Cinco Ranch?" asks Nelson.

"In reality, no. The great thing about Houston is that we have found a way to accommodate a wide range of lifestyles and because of this, we see a healthy inner city as well as a growing suburbia. Living inside the city meets the needs of many, but living in the 'burbs meets the needs of many more, and without transportation infrastructure, Houston cannot continue to provide those options. A wide range of housing options and attainability is a critical component that makes Houston the great and welcoming city that it is so well-known for."

— TED NELSON, NEWLAND COMMUNITIES.

WOODY MANN AND THE RACE AGAINST SIMON

Home builders and community developers weren't the only ones tracking the new trail of the Grand Parkway. Retail soon followed.

Real estate entrepreneur Woody Mann of Houston-based Vista Companies was one of the first to recognize the potential of the Grand Parkway. As the first homes were occupied on the prairie, residents of the area were driving twenty miles just to shop for groceries. Mann decided to do something about it. "A number of years ago, when we were developing a project in a rather under-developed area, one of our bankers told me — 'you know what happens to pioneers — they get arrows in their back,'" he recalled.

"Fortunately, we have been blessed to avoid too many arrows. If you study the growth patterns of most cities and towns, for some inexplicable reason the majority of them tend to grow west and north. Houston is no exception to that phenomenon, so it didn't take a rocket scientist to figure out that the far West Houston/Katy area was going to be area of substantial growth for a number of reasons — mainly the number of master planned communities on the horizon and the attraction of the nationally acclaimed Katy Independent School District. In addition, when we really began to study the demographics of that particular submarket, it was very obvious that there was a substantial amount of untapped purchasing power in the area, based on above-average annual household income, and a real void in specialty retail shopping options — in other words, the area was severely "under-stored." The suburban population was growing and Cinco Ranch was being expanded to eight thousand acres."

— WOODY MANN, VISTA COMPANIES

In the late 1980s Mann began planning for LaCenterra at Cinco Ranch, which eventually became a 34-acre Main Street-centered development of shops, restaurants, office space, and mid-rise multifamily that became the de facto downtown of Cinco Ranch.

"When we bought the original 18-acre tract in 2003, our initial plan was to do a grocery-anchored shopping center at that location," said Mann.

"However, Ted Nelson convinced us to 'think outside the box' and create something that could be a magnet, not only for the entire Cinco Ranch community, but the other surrounding master-planned communities such as Grand Lakes and Seven Meadows as well. Marc Boucher and his team at Boucher Design Group, did an excellent job in designing a true mixed-use, Texas-themed project that has evolved into being a town center development for the entire Katy-area community. Our biggest concern at the time was that [shopping center developer] Simon owned a 130-acre tract at the northeast corner of I-10 and the Grand Parkway, which they intended to develop into a large outdoor center called The Grande. We knew we couldn't compete with Simon, and a number of the prospective tenants we were talking to at the time were also talking to Simon about their project as well. Several of those prospects – who later became our first tenants at LaCenterra – advised us that we needed to build a larger project to create more critical mass in order to have more of a market impact, so we bought an additional 16 acres from Newland which allowed us to substantially increase the LaCenterra footprint to over 400,000 square feet of retail and office space."

— WOODY MANN

With the greater mass, Mann won the market and Simon scrapped their plans for The Grande.

Construction of LaCenterra started in 2006 with the first phase completed the following year and the final phases finished in 2017. Martin Fein Interests added The Grand at LaCenterra, a four-story, 217-unit apartment community. An 18-hour a day activity center was born. Today, LaCenterra also offers a public park — Central Green — opened through a partnership with Willow Fork Drainage.

Late in 2017, Mann's exit strategy arrived in the form of an institutional investor. Mann's Vista Companies, along with partner Denver-based Amstar Group, decided to sell LaCenterra to PGIM Real Estate, an arm of Prudential Financial. The sales price was not officially disclosed, but Colliers International places it at $143.4 million. It meant Mann created $350 per square foot of value on the Grand Parkway — enough to inspire a lot of copycat developers.

Today, the Grand Parkway — now complete from near Rosenberg on the southwest side of Houston to the Kingwood area in the northeast — is where most of Houston's new retail development is occurring. "In Houston and in Texas, retailers are comfortable with freeway locations," explains Jason Gaines, senior vice president and retail division leader with NAI Partners. "We're a freeway state. Retailers feel most comfort when they can come out to Grand Parkway. Retail construction along the Grand Parkway is driven by major category killers — Walmart, Target, Costco — and developers are reacting to that."

The Grand Parkway opened up what retailers really wanted — an area where significant projects could be constructed. "The Grand Parkway gave all the retailers a 'thumbs up' site that they could get excited about and say, 'I want to be there!' It makes the decision-making process much easier," he says.

Gaines added that a lot of the Grand Parkway retail, at least on the newer parts of the roadway, is in the pioneering stages. "There are retailers that specifically want freeway/highway locations, and the Grand Parkway provides that," Gaines says.

Along the Grand Parkway, more than three million square feet of retail, restaurant, and entertainment space is under construction or in the pipeline for completion by 2021, according to 2018 analysis by CBRE Research and GIS Location Intelligence.

The new Grand Parkway retail space, like the homes that preceded it, won't be close to the urban core of the city. The new Grand Parkway-inspired development will be twenty-five or thirty miles from Downtown Houston. And Houston gets bigger and wider.

WHERE ARE THE CITY LIMITS?

In 2014, the Greater Houston Partnership unveiled a new slogan to market the city. When people learned that a new marketing campaign was coming, it was hard to imagine promotional efforts could get any worse. After all, the nation's fourth largest city had survived some unfortunate image campaigns in the past. Who could forget "Houston's Hot" and "Expect the Unexpected" — the marketing slogans that pointed to one of the city's greatest weaknesses and/or carried no meaning at all?

Even average Houstonians who never thought about marketing the city, groaned or emitted a derisive chuckle when they heard prior slogans.

On national level, Houston had little or no name identification. If Houston ever crossed the mental radar screen of the average Americans at all, it was probably in a clichéd repetition of: "Houston, We Have a Problem," a comment voiced by Tom Hanks in the Apollo 13 movie from 1995.

So the bar was low while the new city marketing plan was under development. When the day of the great unveil arrived — June 3, 2014 — the Greater Houston Partnership offered the new municipal sales pitch: "Houston: The City With No Limits."

The slogan, the promoters said, highlighted that Houston was a city with infinite possibilities, a place where innovators created the first domed stadium or completed the first artificial heart transplant. At first blush, the slogan sounded fine. But on second thought, it became obvious the new slogan could be interpreted as a reference to one of the big knocks against Houston — the sin of sprawl.

The "Greater Houston" area, as the Houston-The Woodlands-Sugar Land metropolitan statistical area is called, covers some 10,062 square miles, which is larger than New Jersey. Being a size XXL, Houston is always open to "fat shaming" about its girth, width, and breadth. Even when Houston went through its dark days of Harvey, the critics from around the nation piled on with instant sprawl critiques, blaming Houston's flooding to growth of the suburbs – even though no city in the world was equipped to handle 50 inches of rain in four days.

Over the years, Houston missed mass transit opportunities that could have altered growth patterns and improved mobility as the option of building commuter rail was passed over. The Katy Freeway tragedy — ignoring the existing rail right-of-way on the north side of the freeway and opting to build one of the world's widest freeways instead — may have been the biggest error ever committed by Houston leadership.

So the future growth coming to Houston will have to be propped up by the Grand Parkway and the city's freeway spokes. Infill development can make a small dent on the city's commuting problems, but it won't be enough. Growth in future decades will go to outlying districts, such as Waller County even father to the west. E-commerce retailers will be pushed to the rim for their big box distribution buildings.

The future will bring more retailers like Amazon, which recently built a million-square-foot fulfillment center in Brookshire, west of Houston. And the future will bring more outlying communities like The Woodlands Hills, a new 2,000-acre Howard Hughes community in the Willis area, which lies some forty miles north of downtown Houston. The Woodlands Hills is thirteen miles north of The Woodlands — the original version (established in the early 1970s) that was once considered insanely remote because it is twenty-seven miles north of downtown.

The Houston metropolis is reaching a milestone — development will be thick from Willis on the north, to Galveston on the south, a distance of some one hundred miles. Without the Grand Parkway, this growth could not have happened.

As the city spreads, the workforce is influencing companies to relocate their offices to the suburbs, says office leasing specialist Jon Silberman, managing partner of NAI Partners. With commute times approaching one hour on bad days, working in an office in Downtown or the Inner Loop can be repulsive for residents of the outer suburbs. This prompts companies to relocate their offices to the suburbs, Silberman says, and the exodus will put pressure on downtown landlords.

Case in point: Occidental Petroleum Corporation's plan to move to the Energy Corridor in West Houston, vacating its offices in Greenway Plaza in the Inner Loop. OXY leaves behind 814,000 square feet of office space in Greenway Plaza, a huge amount of space offered for sublease and big enough to be a drag on the city's office market. The decentralization of the workforce, the construction of office buildings in the far suburbs, and the development of communities near the Grand Parkway — it all spreads the city away from Houston's inner core.

The city's population growth continues and Houston continues to expand. Where will it stop? It won't. Metropolitan areas spread upward and outward. The other cities in Texas expand as well. In late 2018, the Houston Chronicle launched Texas Inc., a publication dedicated to covering "business and enterprise in what can be counted as the world's tenth largest economy," wrote Houston Chronicle Business Editor Al Lewis in introducing the new section. The Texas-focused publication launched as what Texans are beginning to realize: It's not far from West Houston to East Austin, and the distance grows shorter every day as the state's metropolitan areas expand. Texas' major markets will never merge, but they will move closer together with links of commerce.

Future generations can await the fulfillment of the concept that is inevitable — the full emergence of the Texas Triangle, a fast-growth, hard-pumping, economic heart connecting the largest cities in the Lone Star State — Houston, Dallas-Fort Worth, Austin, and San Antonio.

6

HIGHRISE SURGE: HOUSTONIANS WITHOUT YARDS – OR CARS

THE RESULTS of a survey shocked the developer of a thirty-seven-story apartment tower in downtown Houston. The amazing fact demonstrated that Houston was changing. Urban high-rise living had taken hold of the market, the survey of the tower's residents showed. The shocker: One-fourth of his tower's residents do not own a car. That does not sound like stereotypical auto-addicted Houstonians. For that matter, neither do high-rise residential towers.

But the popularity of high-rise residential projects has surged in Houston in recent years as baby boomers and millennials have opted for multifamily in droves. The high-rise construction boom has been centered in downtown Houston, Midtown, Montrose, Galleria/Uptown, and a bit westward to the Memorial City area. The new high-rise dwellers can often avoid suburban commutes while being closer to cultural amenities and popular Inner Loop restaurants. So they move close-in. And they move up.

Consider the new high-rise developed by Hines in downtown: Aris Market Square, a thirty-two-story residential tower on the edge of Houston's Theater District overlooking historic Market Square — Houston's first urban park that covers about one-and-a-half acres. The residential tower boasts 274 apartments ranging in size from 570 to 2,227 square feet. A development of Houston-based Hines, Aris — designed by Ziegler Cooper Architects — offers a private "secret garden" — a pocket park, accessible by residents and patrons of Aris' 9,100-square-foot food hall. Designed to be reminiscent of the tree-shaded courtyards in the New Orleans French Quarter, the park has access to Metro Rail and the city beyond.

Hines founder Gerald D. Hines felt strongly that the area between two buildings should be a park that residents could use and that could become part of public realm. Carving out little niches of public space for the creation of the park was an added touch, said architect Scott Ziegler, senior principal at the Urban Residential Studio of Houston-based Ziegler Cooper Architects.

"It wasn't necessary, but we did it to improve the quality of life," Ziegler explained. "Aris Market is Hines' first residential high rise in the CBD and Hines made a strong commitment to building a high-quality urban residential and mixed-use project. There has been a paradigm shift toward urban densification, and Hines sees this type of development as their future. Houston is still in early stages of densification right now."

Aris Market Square — which opened in downtown Houston in 2017 right after Hurricane Harvey — and a number of other high-rise projects in Space City are seeking to change Houston's habit of furthering urban sprawl by densifying the city.

> "I find it very telling that Hines Aris Market Square is constructed on less than one acre of land and provides a home for three hundred residences," says Ziegler, "yet if three hundred single family homes were built in suburban Houston, it would require seventy-five acres of land and twenty-nine miles of roads to service the homes. The twenty-first century challenge for architects will be to undo the damage caused by suburban sprawl and search for development patterns with higher density."

Densification of Houston is occurring via multifamily high-rises downtown and elsewhere around the city. Aris is but one of a number of residential high rises that are planned, under development or recently completed downtown — an area that for years hadn't reported significant new residential construction.

> "There are more high rises under construction today and more on the way," says veteran multifamily analyst Bruce McClenny, president of ApartmentData.com, an information supplier to the multifamily industry. "Since 2013, the number of apartments being built has increased dramatically. There are almost two thousand more high-rise units under construction to be delivered into supply during 2019 and 2020. Plus, there are 3,500 high-rise units as proposed or planned construction."

The two-year pace is more than the high-rise construction total for the entire ten-year period beginning in 2001. Those statistics only include buildings with ten stories of more and don't even touch the many mid-rise developments of less than ten stories.

Houston-based Camden Property Trust is building a twenty-story, 275-unit residential tower in downtown next to the Toyota Center arena, where the Houston Rockets play NBA basketball. It is the company's first ground-up high rise constructed in Houston. Camden has a second downtown tower planned.

> "I think downtown Houston will continue to densify. If you look at Houston from a density perspective, we're one of the least dense cities in America — even less dense than Dallas," said Ric Campo, CEO of Camden, a publicly traded firm that owns more than one hundred sixty apartment complexes with over fifty-thousand apartment homes across the nation. "Over the next ten years, Houston is supposed to add a million more people,

so density is going to increase. Inside the loop is becoming denser and downtown, too. The land downtown has become more expensive and multifamily developments will be denser. Up until now, Camden has built mainly mid-rise developments. Rents have risen enough to support high-rise development."

Downtown rental rates target the upscale market with many one-bedroom units priced at $2,500 or more per month. Two-bedroom apartments can draw more than $4,000 a month in some properties.

Campo, a community leader who has had a long history of downtown civic development, noted that the area is adding more attractions to lure residents downtown. "Over last five to six years, we've had massive investment downtown of over $5 billion," he continued. "There have been continuous efforts by civic leaders to bring people downtown, for Houston to become a twenty-four-hour city. Incentives are part of the equation and include the Downtown Living Initiative, where the city provided incentives to developers to build multifamily downtown. Some three thousand units have been built [recently] or are under construction downtown."

Campo adds that the costs of building associated with land and construction are rising. "It's hard to build low-rise wood construction downtown, so you have to go higher to make economic sense," he said.

Camden's new tower is part of building a stronger downtown, agreed Ziegler. "It's taken a long time for Houston to develop new high quality downtown living," Ziegler continued. "Five years ago, there were probably only 1,500 households downtown. Now there are five thousand plus."

Most Houstonians would agree that downtown Houston has undergone massive changes over the past decade. From a downtown where the sidewalks seemed to roll up at six o'clock and a place only a few thousand residents lived, downtown Houston has been transformed with new multifamily developments and expansive amenities, such as Discovery Green park.

One of the pioneers of downtown residential development is Marvy A. Finger of The Finger Companies. He is a native Houstonian who built his first multifamily development in Houston more than a half century ago. Finger developed the thirty-seven-story One Park Place in 2005. He followed that with 500 Crawford, a four hundred-unit downtown project, completed in early 2016 — just about the time oil prices dipped below thirty dollars a barrel amid a softening Houston economy.

"500 Crawford was a struggle from the first day and continues to be a struggle, but we are at ninety percent occupancy," said Finger. "We were there pretty early. We were the 'first-est with the most-est.' What attracts tenants to downtown residential towers is being able to stroll from their home to a grocery store or a restaurant. Walkability is everything," continued Finger. "This was a shocker for me, but at One Park Place, we found out about twenty-five percent of 650 people — twenty-five percent! — have no car. They have sold their one automobile because they don't need it or don't want it."

Finger believes downtown Houston needs more restaurants and more bars. He predicts another grocery store or two will be added to the urban mix soon.

Houston's multifamily market, including high rises, has been on a roller-coaster ride over the past eighteen months. The market was relatively soft until Hurricane Harvey hit, then much of the multifamily sector vacancy disappeared overnight.

"Although a tragic event, Hurricane Harvey provided the Houston multifamily market a much-needed boost in recovery, said Stuart Showers, director of research at Transwestern. "With high population and job growth in the metro area, market fundamentals will continue to set the stage for the sector to perform well for the balance of the year. As Houston continues to see signs of economic recovery from the energy downturn, the multifamily sector will continue to see growth in effective rents and construction activity."

As those Harvey renters move back into their homes, Houston's occupancy scenario is changing again. The strong job growth reported in 2018 prompted developers to accelerate construction plans. The apartment market suffered through rough times when oil prices dropped sharply in 2014, a downturn that continued for two years, followed by a slow recovery. Houston's weak job market prompted apartment developers to retreat.

The local economy whipped the multifamily market into wild unpredictable gyrations after the oil slump. The year 2017 began with a better economic outlook as Houston hosted Super Bowl LI, which generated a net impact of $347 million for the local economy, according to Rockport Analytics. Then, Houston received two other economic surprising stimuli in 2017 — the World Series run by the world-champion Houston Astros and Hurricane Harvey. From the home games of the play-offs and the World Series, economic spending of twenty million dollars to thirty million dollars was circulated throughout the economy, according to Patrick Jankowski, of the Greater Houston Partnership. Hurricane Harvey flipped the multifamily market overnight. The storm damaged more than one hundred thousand homes and thousands of apartment units. In the days that followed, apartment leasing went on a spree the likes of which had never been seen before.

"From September [2017] through the end of the year, Harvey propelled overall rents by twenty-seven dollars per month and occupancy by 1.7 percentage points. In areas where the most damage to single-family homes occurred, rent and occupancy increases were most pronounced," McClenny said. "In the Energy Corridor, rent rose by eighty-four dollars per month and occupancy gained five percentage points."

While Harvey produced abnormal conditions for the city's apartment market, eventually the homeowners moved back into their repaired homes. Normalcy returned. The development pipeline began flowing again. By the time the one-year anniversary of Hurricane Harvey rolled around in August 2018, forty apartment complexes were under construction in the Greater Houston area and sixty-eight more projects were proposed.

Demand for high-rise units remains high. Developers have built a significant amount of high-rise apartment towers for economic reasons and to meet growing demand. "One reason is that the very high cost of land (over one hundred dollars per square foot in most cases) has forced developers to decrease the footprint and to increase the density of units for a project in the urban core," said McClenny. "Another reason comes from the baby boom generation downsizing, avoiding taxes, upkeep, and repairs. This generation is best suited to handle the high rents of these projects."

Even real estate companies that haven't built multifamily properties before are getting into the act. Shopping center developer Weingarten Realty Investors is constructing The Driscoll At River Oaks, a thirty-story residential high rise offering over three hundred units for lease. Residents of the tower will live within walking distance of shops, restaurants and a Kroger in River Oaks Shopping Center. The tower will also be home to an estimated ten thousand square feet of ground floor retail.

. . .

New high-rise residential projects include:

- Madison Marquette, formerly known as PMRG, completed a forty-story multifamily rental development at 2929 Weslayan. Wade Bowlin, president of the group's Central Division, said leasing at the building, designed by RTKL of Baltimore, has been going very well. "We are currently ninety-two percent and have stayed near capacity for the past two years. 2929 Weslayan delivered product that had never been seen and has achieved the highest [rental] rates in the city. Our latest multifamily development just broke ground in Houston's Midtown district." Madison Marquette's new Midtown tower, 3300 Main, will include three hundred twenty-eight units and ground-floor retail.
- Caydon, an Australia-based developer, is building a two hundred million-dollar, twenty-seven-story multifamily tower at 2850 Main Street. Named "2850," the project has 360-degree views and features 357 units. First residents are expected by August 2019, with completion three months later. Units range from 550 square feet to 1,200 square feet. Designed by Ziegler Cooper Architects, the 342,000-square-foot apartment tower is the first US project for the Melbourne, Australia, firm.
- In a joint venture with TH Real Estate, an affiliate of Nuveen and the Zimmerman family, Hines is developing the thirty-four-story Residences at La Colombe d'Or, a 285-unit high-rise multifamily development in the Montrose/Museum District neighborhood. Designed by Munoz + Albin architects, the tower will have an art gallery and an outdoor plaza with a fireplace. The La Columbe d'Or is next door to Hanover Montrose, a thirty-one-story apartment

tower that was recently developed at 3400 Montrose Boulevard. just south of Westheimer Road.

With help from significant architectural talent, the market for selling high-rise condominiums rose to a new level in the late 1970s. Houston developer Giorgio Borlenghi of the Interfin Corporation, began erecting a huge entry onto the high-rise condo market — Four Leaf Towers, a pair of 40-story buildings in the Galleria area. Interfin retained then-relatively unknown architect Cesar Pelli, who came up with a design in reddish tints borrowed from the brick and terra cotta of the nearby neighborhood. The 400-unit Four Leaf Towers was completed in 1982, shortly before the Houston economy went into a tailspin. Some of the Four Leaf inventory was converted into rental homes, but the units reportedly sold briskly when they returned to the sales market years later. Pelli, the Four Leaf architect, went on to a distinguished career, winning the Gold Medal for lifetime achievement from the American Institute of Architects in 1995.

By the mid-1990s, the high-rise condo was strengthening as demographic trends took hold. In a 1997 interview with the Houston Chronicle, high-rise Realtor Edith Personette said: "People are moving in from the suburbs. I think we are seeing the first wave of baby boomers moving into the empty-nester era."

In the Uptown-Galleria area in the 2000s, Borlenghi continued to build high-rise residential condo towers including Montebello, a thirty-story tower on three acres and its sister property, Villa d'Este — a twenty-seven-story tower on a six-acre, park-like setting atop the banks of Buffalo Bayou.

Borlenghi's latest development, Belfiore, a twenty-six-story building with forty-six units starting at 4,600 square feet, had an average price of $2.8 million; all of the Belfiore units except one were sold before the building opened in 2016. While the city's high-rise condominium market remains robust, Borlenghi is turning his attention to multifamily rentals. "We're seeing more and more individuals whose children have left the nest wanting to downsize and simplify their lives," Borlenghi continues. "They are attracted by a more urban lifestyle but would rather rent, at least initially, without having to make a large financial commitment. We see a great opportunity, thanks to our expertise and reputation for luxury buildings, to satisfy the needs of this market."

At this point, one of the larger market segments is the empty nesters who are downsizing and cashing out of their big homes, agrees Ziegler. "Five years ago, you couldn't talk them into renting, but now apartments are as nice — or nicer — than condos going up," he continues. "The urban amenities have become more sophisticated and we are designing more stylish buildings. Twenty years ago, millennials and young professionals weren't a factor. Now, urban living is all about simplifying our lifestyle, unloading the maintenance burden of a home and moving into an apartment with a concierge to attend to their every wish."

In downtown Houston, real estate entrepreneur Randall Davis helped set the groundwork for high-rise living and loft conversions by bringing the glamour back to the landmark Rice Hotel. More than a century old, the Rice — named after Rice University benefactor William Marsh Rice — was built on the land that was the site of the old Capitol of the Republic of Texas before it was moved to Austin. Mick Jagger and Richard M. Nixon were among the hotel's guests; President John F. Kennedy spent the day there before traveling to Dallas where he was assassinated. The thousand-room Rice Hotel faded and it was declared unsafe and closed in 1977.

The old hotel became an eyesore. It was frequented by the homeless, much to the dismay of real estate professionals like Mark Russell, now vice chairman of Newmark Knight Frank, but who previously spent years leasing office space in the nearby seventy-five-story JP Morgan Chase Tower. The presence of an abandoned Rice Hotel was a downtown blight that seemed like it would never be healed. The Rice sat empty for eighteen years until Davis and Post Properties began a historic renovation of the boarded-up structure, converting the building to more than three hundred lofts, with street-level restaurants. Davis went on to build numerous other high-rise projects in Houston — in addition to converting old warehouses into trendy lofts, including the Hogg Palace Lofts and the Dakota Lofts. Davis is currently overseeing the development of two high-rise condominiums: the Marlowe downtown and the Arabella in the Galleria area. Davis, it should be noted, has demonstrated the spunk, chutzpah, and tenacity to promote urban living in Houston for decades, even when the market was thin.

While suburban single-family housing has great appeal for thousands of families seeking more affordable shelter, people are moving back to the city. Many millennials of today have no desire to live in the suburbs.

> "Maybe when they have kids they will move back to the suburbs, but now they want to be where the action is — near clubs and restaurants, music, museums and ballparks," says Ziegler. "The shift in this mindset is a result of freeway gridlock and the desire for quality of life. Some people spend an hour commuting to and from work every day. Now they desire to live in what we call the twenty-minute bubble — twenty minutes to get to the office, the grocery store, restaurants, and back home again. Suburban development is chewing up our natural environment, covering land with roofs and concrete slabs, causing the flooding problems. I believe if development in Houston had not sprawled outward covering acres of land with impervious surfaces, Houston wouldn't have had Harvey's historic flooding that occurred last year."

The low-density sprawl model of Houston today is unsustainable because of high infrastructure costs – Houston cannot afford to maintain roads, freeways, utility districts, emergency medical service, and fire protection with low-density development, Ziegler says. Today, Houston's city limits encompass six hundred square miles of land. This means Houston has 5.9 people per acre in the city, Ziegler says. The density gets weaker if the outlying areas — Houston's Metropolitan Statistical Area — is included. By comparison, San Francisco has twenty-nine people per acre, New York has 45 and Paris has 82 people per acre. "This is an absurd lack of resourcefulness, and we can't continue to support that," Ziegler said.

Anyone driving around the Inner Loop of Houston instinctively knows density has increased in recent years. Street traffic is heavier. Stores are crowded. Land prices are rising, dictating the necessity for more multifamily and more high-rise development. In the end, Houston cannot avoid its destiny as a dense metropolis. It's just a matter of how quickly it will occur. In the decades ahead, Houston will have it all — a dense urban core and suburbs that expand till kingdom come.

7

THE MARKETING GENIUS OF THE ENERGY CORRIDOR

HOUSTON, the city created by the Allen brothers, a pair of world-class property promoters, has a phenomenal legacy of real estate marketing. The Astrodome, River Oaks, and The Woodlands represent long-lasting project branding that could endure for centuries.

Another place that has earned respect in the world of marketing is the Energy Corridor — a stretch of West Houston that is home to dozens of major oil and gas firms and other companies that service the energy sector. The Energy Corridor's fame resonates in the Middle East, Europe, and Asia.

Truly, the creation of the Energy Corridor moniker is one of the most brilliant strokes in the history of Houston real estate marketing. Beyond the marketing alone, the Energy Corridor is a very tangible, very massive collection of commercial properties, hotels, homes, and retail space.

If the creation of the Energy Corridor could be credited to a single person, it would be David S. Wolff, chairman and president of Wolff Companies. In the 1970s and 1980s, Wolff started and marketed this business district in an area that a mere four decades earlier was mainly farmland.

Wolff is considered by many as the "father" of Houston's

Energy Corridor, a hub that an estimated three hundred multinational, national, and local companies now call home. With nearly a hundred thousand employees, the Energy Corridor, located about fifteen miles from downtown Houston, is the third largest employment center in the region. Strictly defined, the Energy Corridor is more formerly known as Harris County Improvement District Number Four — a special government entity empowered to levy commercial taxes within its boundaries to support investments in infrastructure, urban planning, and branding. The district was created by the Texas Legislature in 2001. The Energy Corridor includes more than 1,700 acres extending along both sides of Interstate 10 from Kirkwood to west of Barker Cypress, and along Eldridge Parkway from north of Interstate 10 to south of Briar Forest, although the de facto boundaries of the Corridor extend far beyond the official borders.

"While David [Wolff] denies he coined the phrase 'The Energy Corridor,' the name is generally attributed to him," said David W. Hightower, executive vice president of development at Midway and Wolff's former executive vice president and chief development officer. "He certainly has been its longest advocate and participant in its evolution. In the mid-1970s he started the Park 10 development, realizing the area was ideally suited for commercial development. It was convenient to new entry-level and move-up housing communities to the northwest, west, and southwest — and to the Memorial neighborhoods where many upper level energy company executives live."

Promoted as a unique suburban environment surrounded by more than twenty-six thousand acres of parks, bayous, and reservoirs, and more than fifty miles of trails, the area "is the place where energy works, lives, and flows. And where energy moves," according to the Energy Corridor District.

Real estate entrepreneurs knew about the area in the 1970s but mostly declined to pursue development because they felt the Addicks and Barker Reservoirs would be a barrier to growth. Not David Wolff. He believed real estate development would leapfrog the Addicks and Barker and that the reservoirs would ultimately be considered a major attraction, providing twenty-six thousand acres of open park space in an area that would eventually become densely populated.

A Philadelphia native who earned a master's degree in business administration from Harvard Business School in 1964, Wolff arrived in Houston with fresh perspective. Wolff was keenly aware of Houston's traditional westward growth, as well as Katy Freeway access and the availability of large tracts of land both inside and west of State Highway 6 — the closer-in tracts for corporate campuses. Wolff also noticed a tendency of the business community that was probably the most important characteristic of them all: The preponderance of decision-making executives resided in the adjacent Memorial area on the west side of town.

> "We went out there because we felt there was an opportunity to develop a light industrial park along the Katy Freeway," Wolff recalled. "Starting in 1972, my then-partner — Niel Morgan — and I were able to assemble fifteen contiguous properties totaling five hundred and fifty acres with 2.6 miles of freeway frontage extending all the way from Highway 6 west to Barker-Cypress Road. This became Park 10. It, in essence, was the connection between the land east of the reservoirs and the land to the west. The land was separated from the freeway by a railroad track."

Wolff and Morgan made some significant moves to improve

the property, including creating an east-west street called Park Row.

Wolff was especially attracted by the difference in prices inside (east of) Highway 6 and outside (west of) Highway 6 — $38,000 per acre inside versus $10,000 per acre west of 6. Wolff had seen a lot of marginal, earlier development closer-in on Katy Freeway, and felt there eventually would be a demand for larger, higher quality uses as development moved west into the new, unspoiled area. "Our initial selling prices were under one dollar a square foot," said Wolff.

> "Users such as M.W. Kellogg's Research Center acquired sites in Park 10 and prices soon increased to $1.50 and two dollars for service center/flex buildings. Then, more companies such as Star Furniture and Atwood Oceanics came in. Subsequently we were able to attract office users such as PROCON and Morrison-Knudsen. Eventually prices moved up into the ten dollar per square foot range with high-end purchasers, such as the Houston Chronicle as well as suburban office building developers."
>
> — DAVID S. WOLFF, CHAIRMAN AND PRESIDENT OF WOLFF COMPANIES

Four decades later land prices in Park 10 exceed twenty dollars per square foot.

What really made the Energy Corridor take off was that while Wolff was assembling Park 10, Shell Oil acquired two hundred acres from Dairy Ashford to Eldridge, later selling the western half of that to Conoco. Exxon Chemical and ARCO soon built their campuses; then Amoco (now BP) developed its towers. "The major oil companies attracted smaller oil companies, engineering firms such as Stone and Webster and Worley-Parsons, drilling companies such as Diamond M, and oilfield service providers such as Schlumberger and McDermott, as the Corridor became a respected and proven location," said Wolff.

Equally important were the very active large scale residential developments taking place on thousands of acres west of the Corridor, such as Cinco Ranch, Kelliwood and Williamsburg.

> "Families were able to buy a new house for two hundred thousand dollars to three hundred thousand dollars in an attractive master planned community and a good school district — and be fifteen minutes from great employment," said Wolff. "The new housing attracted the employers because they knew it would help them attract and retain good employees; and the jobs brought the buyers. It was great synergism with each feeding the other."

Some forty years later Houston's Energy Corridor is considered one of the nation's premier employment centers and boasts the headquarters and regional offices of prominent international energy and energy services firms including BP America, Shell Exploration and Production, ConocoPhillips, CITGO, Dow Chemical, PGS, and Mustang/Wood Group. Non-energy companies including Cardinal Health Care Inc., Sysco Corporation, Gulf States Toyota, and Star Furniture also have a major presence in the Energy Corridor, according to a study by CDS Market Research. CDS added that the Energy Corridor has the capacity for a population of 22,000 and 104,000 jobs based on counts of housing units and commercial square footage, assuming a high occupancy.

Throughout the years as the energy sector endured boom and bust cycles, so did the Corridor. The area suffered in the 1980s as oil prices bottomed out, then recovered just like the energy sector.

Aided by the widespread use of hydraulic fracturing, a drilling method known as fracking, oil production began to take off around 2010 in the so-called Shale Revolution. Energy companies expanded rapidly. By 2013, Class A office space in the Energy Corridor was 99 percent occupied, according to CBRE. The fact that the Energy Corridor was the most dynamic office submarket in the nation did not go unnoticed. Developers responded. Dozens of office buildings were constructed. Then oil prices crashed again. Some of that new office space remained vacant for years. Vacancy rates skyrocketed and sublease space was prevalent. It was quite a fall for the Energy Corridor after being one of the hottest submarkets in the nation to one of the worst.

The recent fracking-era bust that began in late 2014 was perhaps one of the worst downturns in the history of American oil, marked by a drop in the rig count and the drastic reduction of energy-industry capital spending. The timing couldn't have been worse for real estate entrepreneurs. Developers had begun starting buildings in the Energy Corridor like there was no tomorrow. But tomorrow arrived sooner than expected. Faced with a drastic new energy world, companies downsized. Exxon Mobil Chemical left its Energy Corridor facility, relocating to the corporation's new campus in north Houston.

The vibrant Energy Corridor office market slumped as did the price of oil, leaving developers with considerable office vacancy and a large supply of sublease space — and an uncertain future. By the third quarter of 2016, the Energy Corridor had a three million square-foot supply of sublease space — more than any other submarket in the nation, according to JLL. Near the end of 2018 office vacancy was well over twenty percent. If the statistics included unwanted space on the sublease market, the "availability rate" was over thirty-five percent, according to NAI Partners. "There is a high concentration of oil and gas companies that dumped office space on the sublease market and there has been significant new construction," said Dan F. Boyles Jr., a partner in NAI Partners Office Tenant Rep Group.

"Every time we see a downturn in the energy industry which leads to a subsequent downturn in the Houston office market, prognosticators say it will take years to absorb the vacant space. What I have found is that it generally recovers quicker than most think."

— DAN F. BOYLES JR., PARTNER IN NAI PARTNERS OFFICE TENANT REP GROUP

The drop in oil prices hurt the office market the most, particularly the Energy Corridor. It also hit the Westchase and Sam Houston Toll Road West areas, where the companies that are in the exploration and production (E&P) business, as well as the energy services industry, are located. (The Energy Corridor has about twenty-five million square feet of Class A and B office space, according to CBRE; when nearby parts of West Houston are included, the total is well over fifty million square feet.)

"The real driver for office space in the energy industry was companies doing offshore exploration," said Rand Stephens, managing director and principal at Avison Young. "We need the offshore business to come back to see significant absorption of office space. Our research shows some evidence of activity offshore, but we're not ready to say that there's a recovery underway in offshore drilling. Also complicating a recovery in the office market is the increasing trend for companies to use less square footage per employee. So, companies that are expanding will do so using less square footage than in the past. Companies are constantly working to be more efficient by doing more business with less people. As a result, we're seeing companies that are expanding but downsizing in total square footage used. Have we fully recovered? I believe we've bottomed. The question is: What does the recovery look like?"

But before that recovery could begin in earnest, along came Hurricane Harvey — an extraordinary event in the wake of a historic energy bust — abruptly disrupting the operations of numerous companies in the Corridor. The University of Wisconsin called Harvey a thousand-year storm, with no rainfall precedent in the history of North America. Moody's Analytics estimated the cost of Harvey's wrath at between ninety-seven billion dollars and one hundred eight billion dollars. Overall, though, analysts predicted that Harvey wouldn't significantly alter Houston's long-term growth path – since with only a few exceptions, economic growth has been good in Houston.

> "With the energy crisis and now lingering effects from Hurricane Harvey, the Energy Corridor has one of the highest vacancy rates in the city," said Chris Lewis, managing principal at Lee & Associates in Houston. "The large footprint of remaining sublease avails in the submarket are also set to mature in the near future, creating even more potential supply. The Energy Corridor offers great housing and schools, with an office environment close to home; so, we would not anticipate a mass exodus of the market."

For the most part, the Energy Corridor wasn't greatly affected during the five days of relentless rain from the storm. The area experienced extensive inland flooding from Hurricane Harvey after the United States Army Corps of Engineers opened the Addicks and Barker reservoirs in West Houston. Officials became concerned there might be a chance of catastrophic failure at the earthen dams, which were brimming with some 400,000-acre-feet of water — about the same volume of water that flows over Niagara Falls in a week and a half. Tweeted Mayor Sylvester Turner at the time: "US Army Corps of Engineers says water releases into Buffalo Bayou on west side necessary to avoid larger catastrophe in next rain." The reservoir releases resulted in extensive and sustained flooding of residential and commercial areas throughout the Energy Corridor and West Houston.

Perhaps one of the region's most affected properties was the park-like, thirty-five-acre Republic Square site — the former home of Exxon Mobil Chemical Corp. Located just west of Eldridge Road at the western gateway to Terry Hershey Park, the wooded campus boasted prime frontage along Memorial Drive and Interstate 10. Exxon sold the site to Third Palm Capital for more than $70 million just before the economic downturn and oil price decline that began in the last part of 2014. Third Palm Capital, affiliated with Dart Enterprises of the Cayman Islands, rechristened the campus Republic Square and had begun renovating the site in multiple phases and planned to constructing new buildings.

The new owners sought to attract an array of locally owned small businesses, international companies seeking a Houston presence and incubators including Houston Technology Center. Dozens of leases had been signed for Republic Square's 320,000 square feet of space — the majority being small businesses and tech companies. One of Republic Square's most anticipated new offerings was 20,000 square feet of Workstyle-branded collaborative space. Third Palm Capital was also finalizing plans to convert 10,000 square feet of former ground-floor office space into dog-friendly, flexible office and artist studio space.

Those plans were thrown into disarray by Hurricane Harvey.

Republic Square's meeting and event center was hit the hardest and was demolished. The main building weathered the storm fairly well — no flooding on the first floor — but the basement garage where all the mechanicals were located took in all the water.

In prior economic downturns, the Energy Corridor was typically the first to be hit and the quickest to recover. "It mirrors the energy business itself," said Tyler Garrett, vice president for the Houston office division of Transwestern. "True, there might not be as many jobs as before, but production is higher now than it has ever been."

Garrett added that the energy downturn caused a massive focus on efficiency in the oil and gas business. "That, coupled with technology, has led to a simple result — it takes fewer people than before to produce oil and gas both at the well and in the office," he said. "The downturn was preceded by a buildup of hiring that then had to reverse itself for the companies to stay afloat."

Midway's Hightower believes the corridor is already recovering. "I don't believe the flooding has had a long term or lingering negative impact," he continued. "Obviously, it had a short-term impact, but the market is coming back. There have been several sizable leases announced," And Occidental (OXY) is purchasing the former ConocoPhillips campus at the northeast corner of I-10 and Eldridge. That is a major indication that the future of the Corridor is very positive."

The Energy Corridor's multifamily sector is beginning to get active again in the region; several hotels have been added to the market in the last few years and there are other operators looking for sites, Hightower said. He added that retail is always going to be a challenge because of the reservoirs, but as more multifamily is added, more retail and restaurants will open.

"I think we will continue to see the Corridor become denser," said Hightower. "We are already seeing some of the early light industrial buildings built in the 1970s in Park 10 demolished and new office buildings and other higher uses replace them. And I think we will see other industries grow in the corridor that may serve the energy companies there, but that are not so reliant on the energy industry."

The factors that made the Energy Corridor attractive during the initial phases are those that will prevail today, believes

Wolff, the father of the Corridor. "Conoco is moving from its present campus at the northeast corner of I-10 and Eldridge to two new towers developed by Trammell Crow totaling about 1 million square feet at the southwest corner of that intersection," said Wolff. "Transocean is also coming from Greenway to fully occupy a new 300,000 square-foot building on Eldridge." As supporting evidence of sustained strength, Wolff named several energy-related firms that have made recent commitments to expand in the area: Marathon Oil, Schlumberger, Saudi Aramco and Air Liquide.

Still, there is an identity crisis of sorts, or at least an identity competition. Success brings imitation and the Energy Corridor has admirers. Exxon Mobil, Southwestern Energy, Anadarko, and other energy firms have established a major presence on the north side of Houston and some have tried to promote the Spring/Woodlands areas as the "New Energy Corridor" or the "Second Energy Corridor." Exxon Mobil's new north-side campus has had a big impact on the area and a demand has built among companies that want to be close to it, said Boyles of NAI Partners, adding that the major relocations there such as the American Bureau of Shipping and Hewlett Packard were not because of Exxon Mobil.

> "Those companies came because they were drawn by the amenity base there including Springwoods Village as well as the increased access provided by the completion of the Grand Parkway," said Boyles. "In my opinion, the area is not going to surpass what you see on the west side of town. The underlying drivers are infrastructure, access, and amenities, not Exxon Mobil and Anadarko. Look at Houston. The master planned communities are on the west side and north side and a lot in between, so major corporations are trying to figure out a way to get near to them."

Wolff agrees, pointing out the original Energy Corridor is adding to the critical mass at this time and it is diversifying. Non-energy companies such as food supplier Sysco Corporation and regional auto distributor Gulf States Toyota Inc. have major headquarters in the area. A new two-hundred-million-dollar healthcare facility by MD Anderson joins Methodist and Texas Children's hospitals. Will the diversity tarnish the Corridor's identity? "Whether in the future it is called the Energy Corridor or the 'downtown of West Houston' is not important," Wolff said. "The attraction is still the same: accessibility, job formation, desirable new housing, and attractive school districts."

The West Houston region is working on quality of life issues with the Energy Corridor Improvement District. Initiatives include the 550-acre Terry Hershey Park and important amenities, such as multifamily housing, mixed-use developments including Midway's CityCentre, and a new campus for the University of Houston.

> "There are a lot of great things continuing to add to the vibrancy of the area," said Wolff. "As Houston continues to move west to the Brazos River, the Energy Corridor's location — which I now define as extending from Memorial City to Barker-Cypress — will become even more central."

Also aiding in the Energy Corridor's recovery is the fact that Houston's economy has come a long way since Hurricane Harvey, said Martin Fein, chief executive officer of Martin Fein Interests Ltd. "We have created some hundred thousand jobs in the last twelve months and the city's economic climate feels better than it did a few years ago," said Fein. "Home sales are strong, and we are seeing strong job creation as well as continued recovery in energy sector. Also, a portion of the Houston economy runs parallel to the US economy and the Port of Houston is doing very well, which is also good news."

David Wolff has been developing real estate in Houston for more than fifty years — he came here when the population was two million, compared to today's seven million — "and I tell people that Houston can be a difficult city to predict. But the strength of our city is based on it being an open society which is growth-oriented and optimistic. As long as these factors continue, I share in that optimism."

The holders of optimism will be tested in the decades ahead as will the occupiers of the Energy Corridor buildings. Climate change is expected to push the energy industry toward lowering carbon emissions and reducing energy demand. The next generation of energy companies will adapt. In thirty years, the Energy Corridor name, one of the best-known real estate marketing monikers in Houston's history, may fall into disuse.

But no matter what it's called, this is a major business district with more office space than the downtowns of many moderate-sized cities and it is reasonable to predict additional office buildings will be constructed in the Energy Corridor area sooner than expected.

8

ADAPTIVE REUSE AND HOUSTON'S 72 MILLION SQUARE-FOOT BUBBLE

HOUSTON'S DOWNTOWN buildings are moving toward obsolescence faster than typewriters after the introduction of personal computers. But typewriters were easy to dispose of. Buildings are not.

Downtown Houston has fifty-nine "Class C" buildings with a total of 1.7 million square feet of office space, according to CBRE. Not appropriate for major corporations, the "Class C" buildings are older, less desirable properties with lower rents. As time goes on, office buildings slide down the food chain, from Class A to Class B to Class C. Rental rates fall. Even though the city's vacancy rate is high, work is starting on new office towers in downtown and in the northern and western suburbs. Destiny awaits. Unneeded office space grows. Many landlords are left with unfortunate choices: foreclosure, bulldozer, or implosion.

Rather than summoning the wrecking ball, the option that makes downtown a better place is something developers call "adaptive reuse." In downtown Houston, it usually means turning office buildings into apartments or hotels. The results can be worthwhile. And these transformations may be key to keeping downtown's ventricles throbbing.

Consider a downtown historic building that had declined to

serving as a pizza delivery outpost with plenty of emptiness up above. An ugly demise was ahead — at least that is the way it appeared a decade ago. But over one hundred years ago when the tower opened, the S.F. Carter Building at 806 Main in downtown Houston instantly became one of the city's most remarkable structures — and one of the most prestigious. Built by banker Samuel Fain Carter in 1910, the sixteen-story building boasted an elaborate garden on the roof and bank vault in the basement. Billed as the city's first full-fledged skyscraper, the Carter Building introduced Houstonians to drinking fountains that circulated iced water, air conditioning units throughout the building, and mens' and ladies' wash basins on each floor.

But like all things man-made, the Carter Building didn't age particularly well.

By the twenty-first century, only half its space was occupied. Some of its glass panels had been replaced by sheets of plywood and Domino's pizza was one of the ground floor's major tenants. In the past, developers might have razed the structure and erected an office building double its size. Or they may have turned it into another flat, surface parking lot with no trees. Instead, Pearl Real Estate of Fort Worth — a company specializing in the development, construction, and operation of hotels — purchased the property. With Houston's Downtown Redevelopment Authority providing $12 million in subsidies, the Pearl group spent an additional $80 million converting it into the 328-room JW Marriott hotel.

"The transformation of the one-hundred-year old S.F. Carter Building into the JW Marriott is nothing short of a miracle," said Houstonian William R. Franks, president of William R. Franks Real Estate and an integral player in the makeover. "We started with an old ugly problematic corner building, a 1960s poor attempt at a modernization, stripping all of that cladding, years of cheaply done tenant improvements and doing a complete historical sensitive redevelopment into the National Trust for Historic Preservation Award for the best building of the year. This is what can be accomplished with adaptive reuse, if done correctly."

The project was, in fact, a miracle because Houston is not known for preserving its historical structures. In the 1990s, Franks recalls, a few individuals started the adaptive-reuses movement in a bigger way — making it "cool" to be a historical redeveloper.

"I have a lot of thoughts and feelings about historic rehabilitation to ensure that buildings that are the story of our city and county are allowed to live to be enjoyed by our children and grandchildren for generations to come," Franks said. "Anyone can knock down a building and build a new one, but it lacks the history and importance of some of these major iconic buildings that built our great city. Looking back, I believe the city of Houston wishes it had back some of our history ... like the Shamrock Hotel and others."

Today, renovated structures seem to be as much in demand, Franks continued, citing as one example the Southern Pacific Railroad Building in downtown Houston. "It was a large building that had been occupied by the railroad company since 1910," said Franks, who tackled the redevelopment in the 1990s. "We converted it into Bayou Lofts, a mixed-use development of retail, garage, restaurants, office and high-rise lofts. We were the second largest conversion behind the Rice Hotel. Bayou Lofts is still going strong today."

Adaptive reuse — taking older buildings and renovating them for new possibilities — is now gaining momentum in Houston. In other cities, historic structures that had fallen on tough times were excellent candidates for a makeover, with developers often utilizing tax incentives for historic preservation offered by federal and municipal governments and carefully preserving the architectural character. But the trend was slow to catch on in Houston. Over the years, Houston has not done a good job of keeping its historic structures for another day — and use.

Some of Houston's oldest structures have become parking lots or simply demolished. The city lost much of Houston's character, many citizens believe, because it has demolished or covered up so many of its old structures. Seemingly blind to the benefits that historic buildings contribute in New York, Boston, and elsewhere on the East Coast, Houston's demolition legacy continues as history crumbles and unique character gets hauled off in dump trucks.

The tide is changing.

Michael G. Scheurich, chief executive officer at Arch-Con Corporation, one of the city's most active construction firms, sees redevelopment of existing properties is trending upward. He noted that Arch-Con has completed quite a few adaptive reuse projects and redeveloped several historic buildings.

"There is very limited inventory, and the inventory that would still qualify will take much more imagination to make these projects attractive for adaptive reuse," Scheurich explains. "We are currently working on the AC Marriott in downtown Houston, built in 1914 as the headquarters of Gulf Oil by Houston entrepreneur Jesse Jones. What is particularly exciting about this project is that the ballroom was once a silent movie theater in the early 1900s and will transform into a ballroom and restaurant with a grand barrel ceiling."

Another century-old office tower — which dominated Houston's skyline for thirty-five years — has also been given a new lease on life. Midway and Lionstone Investments have repositioned the JPMorgan Chase Building — formerly the Gulf Building — as well as the neighboring 708 Main structure in a complex renamed The Jones on Main.

The layers of history are deep with early-day tenants that were once pioneers in a fledgling oil industry.

The 708 Main building, constructed in 1908, was once the headquarters of The Texas Company, which later became Texaco. The 712 Main, built in 1927, is a former headquarters of Gulf Oil Co. and on the National Register of Historic Places.

"Historic preservationists consider it one of the most significant examples of Art Deco architecture in the southwestern United States," Chris Seckinger, investment manager at Midway, explained. "Not only is it uniquely beautiful, but its location in the epicenter of a reviving historic district in the CBD is compelling. The Jones on Main enjoys a competitive advantage because the unique nature of the property elevates it above being just another commodity."

It is important for Houston that The Jones on Main remains

relevant and prominent for many years to come, said Damon Thames, vice president at Colvill Office Properties.

"Houston has not always had a reputation for appreciating the value of our architectural masterpieces from another era, but that is changing," continues Thames. "We have seen very strong demand for office space from discerning tenants who are attracted to the strong historic character of both buildings, when combined with desired amenities."

Jones on Main also offers a competitive advantage for today's millennial-driven workforce: one of the highest scores for "bike-ability" in the city. One of the new tenants in the Jones on Main redevelopment is WeWork, a "co-working" facility that leased eighty-six thousand square feet. WeWork is one of a number of shared-office companies that have entered Houston recently. With a reputation for eclectic interiors, collaborative workspace, and fun diversions like ping pong tables, WeWork was a good fit for the historic project.

Preservationists are hoping for more success in the future because of the large supply of Houston's office buildings downtown that are now considered obsolete, or at least in need or major upgrades, lend themselves to creative adaptation.

"Some of them are going to have to be repurposed for new uses," says Dan Bellow, president of JLL Houston. "That happens everywhere, and it's happened in downtown before. Once a building is functionally obsolete and difficult to lease, you've got to think of what else it could be – hospitality, residential, or some other use. If they have good quality locations, then some may turn into land sites for redevelopment. We've seen a lot of that in downtown over the years and it's the case for both towers currently under construction."

"I think we'll see very creative developers find ways to reuse Class C office buildings," says Mark Taylor, senior managing director of the CBRE real estate firm's Houston office. "Class C offices became very good hotels because they are well located. And they have good structural bones."

A diagnosis of the source of Houston's oversupply is easy to identify. "A large portion of Houston's downtown skyline was built in the early eighties. And then the city was hit with a massive downturn in energy and the savings and loan crisis," says Tyler Garrett, vice president for the Houston office division of Transwestern. "Because of that, Houston went over fifteen years without any new office product constructed in the Central Business District as the market slowly turned toward equilibrium."

Aggressive lending and favorable tax treatments ignited a development boom in the early 1980s, giving birth to the Houston's oversupply of office space. In four years alone — 1981 to 1984 — some 71.6 million square feet of office space was constructed in Houston. The space from that four-year surge equates to 34 percent of the market's current inventory, according to CBRE.

In other words, a lot of Houston buildings are aging and renovation is needed soon.

The maturity bubble — as so many buildings reach their fortieth birthday at the same time – will burst. Landlords can spend millions to redevelop or let the buildings decline. Decision time is here. Dozens of landlords will be deciding to transform their buildings to other uses and this will roil the market.

The redevelopment of downtown's aging office stock is the key to making downtown vibrant with more residents, retail and after-hours activity related to convention goers. But more multi-family — with the population increases it brings — is key. The big wave of redeveloping office buildings into residential properties was the "major driver" for reinvigorating downtown Dallas in recent years, says John F. Crawford, vice chairman of Downtown Dallas Inc., a nonprofit advocate for economic development.

Economics play a large role in adaptive reuse, notes Marvy A. Finger, president and chief executive officer of the Finger Companies, one of the city's largest apartment development firms.

> "The cost of conversion sometimes is not favorable," he continued. "Until we start generating greater employment growth — and not just blue collar growth — I don't think conversions make economic sense. When you look at the employment growth numbers in Houston, it's mainly from Port of Houston, Medical Center, petrochemical and refineries, and they cannot afford Class A rent or the required rent of a converted building."

Growth in the upper-end multifamily market must be supported by increasing numbers of Houstonians who want rental housing, Finger says. "Sometimes developers don't look at fundamentals. Their only consideration is 'can I borrow the money?' and 'can I sell the product once I finish it?'"

The economics were right for the adaptive reuse of the historic Stowers Furniture building in downtown Houston. Built in 1913, the ten-story structure at 820 Fannin is now the 173-room Aloft Houston Downtown hotel and listed on the National Register of Historic Places.

"It was important to leverage techniques and processes to protect and restore historical items," said Scheurich, contractor for the Stowers redevelopment. "Historic renovations are known for having a myriad of obstacles, so ensuring the project would stay within the guidelines of historic designation locally and nationally was a rewarding, global challenge. Adding a rooftop pool, the most distinguishing feature, was also the most challenging as it needed to meet not only state, but also federal guidelines."

Continuing its adaptive reuse mode, Arch-Con is also handling the redevelopment of the old Palace Lanes bowling alley on Bellaire Boulevard in Southside Place. "We are reviving this iconic 1955 building with a fantastic history of bowling on the first floor and offices on the second," said Scheurich. "The removal of the entire front façade as well as the second level will create a fresh new look. The second level will be raised by four feet to accommodate modern office design. The first floor will keep to the life and legacy of Palace Bowling Lanes with a reset of retail, restaurant and entertainment... and yes, that does include bowling."

What is historic, and worth saving, however, varies with the beholder. Houston is gradually discovering that "historic" means "old and worth the trouble." That moniker applies to a building that's part of a community's past. Put another way: Old buildings can offer opportunities for a community's future. A city needs old buildings to maintain a sense of permanency and heritage. Older buildings are just more interesting. Outbursts of redevelopment, with projects like Sawyer Yards have given momentum to Houston's Inner Loop districts like EaDo, the Heights and First Ward where industrial buildings have been transformed into retail, restaurants, studios, and creative office space.

But not every old building is a candidate for renewal, emphasized William R. Franks.

"In historic redevelopment you must first study and take all things into consideration of what is the best adaptive reuse for this particular property," Franks added. "Once that is determined, you can head into the due diligence stage to see if it is going to work. Hotels are one product type that suits certain urban historic buildings that are tight, not as large as today's skyscrapers, may not have parking but are in a central demand location. It also may be a building that would not serve as well if rehabilitated back as an office building due to new high-rise competition. But, would make a perfect hotel."

While a number of structures already have been repurposed, the supply may be limited. "I don't think we have as many older, empty buildings as some of the cities in the East," says Martin Fein, chief executive officer of multifamily developer Martin Fein Interests. He notes that redevelopments, although they make more sense in downtown where land prices are higher, have been completed in quality, close-in districts outside of downtown.

> "Already, we've seen several office buildings converted to apartments including an office building in Greenway Plaza and one in the Meyerland area. There may be more in the future; it depends on the market and the specific economics of conversion."
>
> — MARTIN FEIN, CEO, MULTIFAMILY DEVELOPER MARTIN FEIN INTERESTS

History comes alive when an individual not only reads about the past but is also able to experience it. A concerted effort to preserve Houston's heritage is a vital link to the city's cultural, educational, aesthetic, inspirational, and economic legacies — ingredients that quite literally make us who we are. Truly, all history is worth preserving, but sometimes the cost of preservation is so high that demolition is inevitable.

Houston may have already lost the battle for historic preservation. Too many great old buildings have been demolished without a whimper.

Houston will never have a French Quarter like New Orleans or a LoDo like Denver. The most meaningful playing field for the future of the city is downtown Houston and the huge supply of aging buildings built in the early 1980s. The failure to transition these forty-year-old buildings to higher use could deflate downtown and its property values. Houston leaders should not panic, though. There is a firewall of protection from the free-enterprise players in the city. When money can be made by redeveloping older properties, rest assured, Houston developers can sniff out the opportunities.

Real estate entrepreneurship made Houston and it will save it.

9

PARKS: THE CATALYTIC CONVERTER

THE SUPER BOWL, the football game that has become a national holiday, has been held in Houston three times over the years. The first time was in 1974 and it was played in Rice Stadium, a college venue that was big enough to pack in seventy-two thousand fans. Houston's second Super Bowl, played in 2004, is best remembered for its controversial halftime show where Janet Jackson's breast, adorned with a nipple shield, was exposed for about half a second, in what was later referred to as a "wardrobe malfunction."

Houston's third Super Bowl on February 5, 2017, featured a national coming-out-party for a debutante that was a place, not a person. The real star of Houston's third Super Bowl, at least in minds of Houston boosters, was a downtown park.

The third time is a charm, as they say. And Houston leaders pulled out all the stops to make hosting the Super Bowl an opportunity to showcase how much Houston, particularly its downtown, had changed. Fan-oriented activities during the lead-up to Super Bowl LI were centered around Discovery Green, a downtown park that opened in 2008. The unveiling celebration was called Super Bowl Live, a ten-day festival with live concerts and other entertainment, including fireworks. The neighboring

George R. Brown Convention Center hosted the annual NFL Experience event, which featured interactive activities and appearances by players.

Discovery Green park showed the world how America's fourth largest city had transformed a part of its downtown from a concrete desert into an oasis of green, recalls Houston Super Bowl Host Committee Chairman Ric Campo.

> "The 12-acre Discovery Green was the epicenter of Super Bowl Live, and we took another fourteen acres for the event. So, we had a twenty-six-acre footprint during the Super Bowl. We attracted some 1.3 million people over ten days to Discovery Green, creating an amazing vibe in Houston. Only about one hundred fifty thousand of those people were from out of town. We drew a million Houston residents downtown. Some Houstonians have never been downtown, and they were surprised to see offerings such as Discovery Green — a big part of Houston's renaissance. It used to be that east of Main Street was no man's land. But with Discovery Green, the development of Partnership Tower and the George R. Brown Convention Center anchoring area — and the addition of many new restaurants — downtown Houston is becoming more pedestrian friendly and a more desirable for people to visit and live."
>
> — HOUSTON SUPER BOWL HOST COMMITTEE CHAIRMAN RIC CAMPO

After a century as a gray hardscape, Houston's Central Business District is blossoming. The city is becoming greener with new places such as Discovery Green and the enhanced Buffalo Bayou, as well as the nearby more expansive Memorial Park and the revitalized Hermann Park. Houstonians are benefitting from efforts to make the city more beautiful — and pedestrian friendly; the changes are attracting not only new developments downtown but also new residents. High-rise and mid-rise residential construction has increased sharply in recent years.

The Texas Department of Transportation is changing the route of the Gulf Freeway through downtown, allowing the removal of the Pierce Elevated — the big barrier between Houston's downtown and its midtown. "It will create an incredible opportunity to develop green space," Campo says. "The freeway reconstruction would remove barriers from downtown, reconnect communities that were cut off by the old freeways and the area would become more usable and user-friendlier, creating a gateway between downtown and the other surrounding communities. The park and green space would totally transform and connect neighborhoods that have been cut off."

The creation of urban green space creates value in a way that is almost as lucrative as the way the U.S. Mint creates money. The land around the rim of Discovery Green in downtown is covered with new high-rise development.

- The first major project was the Finger Companies' One Park Place, a 346-unit high-end residential tower that opened in 2009.
- It was soon followed by Hess Tower, an office development that proved the value of being located by the park when Canadian investors bought it in 2011 for $442.5 million or $524 per square foot, a record price per square foot for commercial space in Houston at the time.
- In 2017, the thousand-room Marriott Marquis convention hotel opened on the north side of Discovery Green and boosted Houston's convention package, which has the 1,200-room Hilton Americas-Houston.
- In 2011, a nineteen-story Embassy Suites hotel developed by American Liberty Hospitality opened

on Dallas Street, across the street from Discovery Green.

The park-spawned building boom has been significant. Discovery Green is now encircled with over a billion dollars worth of new and recent development.

The creators of Discovery Green did not blindly stumble into success.

"We asked the public what they wanted to see in a park and then delivered on those hopes and dreams, while creating a place that people could enjoy every day and not just for special events," says architect Guy Hagstette, vice president, parks and civic projects at the Kinder Foundation, which helped to create the downtown park. "There was a recognition from the start that the park's location and functions were unique, so it would be difficult for it to fit within a larger parks department. It required plain old hard work and commitment day in and day out by the incredible Discovery Green Conservancy team. Major up-front commitments from generous philanthropists and a long-term funding strategy for maintenance and operations that did not require any resources from our overburdened parks department were identified at the beginning."

Discovery Green is only part of the greening of Houston. One of the other major undertakings is Buffalo Bayou Park, a realization of a century-old vision for parks along Houston's bayous. The land for the park was purchased one hundred years ago, using park bond funds approved by voters in 1912. However, the lack of resources, floods, and a shift in civic priorities caused the vision to falter after World War II. Enter the Buffalo Bayou Partnership (BBP), which has worked tirelessly to resurrect that vision as part of its Buffalo Bayou & Beyond plan in 2002, aided by a significant gift from the Kinder Foundation that turned the plan into reality. "The lessons are one, this work can take time, patience, and hard work over as many as one hundred years," says Hagstette, "and two, we have to be willing to dedicate real funding to our parks."

A massive plan is also underway for the redevelopment of the 1,464-acre Memorial Park — one of the largest urban parks in the country — including a land bridge over heavily traveled Memorial Drive.

> "Like Buffalo Bayou Park, Memorial Park represents a century-old vision that lost steam in the mid-twentieth century," explains Hagstette. "We are finally in a position to realize its potential in a manner that preserves its valuable ecological assets. Ten years from now, Houstonians will be able to get to and around the park much more easily to experience the land bridge, restored prairie ecosystems, Eastern Glades, Memorial Groves, new ball fields, and a timing track for runners. The master plan is incredibly ambitious, and its initial ten-year plan – made possible by a gift from the Kinder Foundation, a commitment from the Uptown Development Authority and additional fundraising by Memorial Park Conservancy — provides the resources to take a huge leap forward."

As Houston continues to grow and likely surpass Chicago in population in coming years, the question is not whether it will grow but how it will grow. "Statistics like population size only tell part of the story," Hagstette explains. "Yes, we want Houston to grow, but we also want Houstonians to be glad they live here and urge their friends and families to move here, too. Parks are truly democratic spaces that all people can enjoy, so investing in them is investing in the future of our entire city."

The drive to improve the city's quality of life is felt throughout the city. Consider Levy Park, just west of Kirby

Drive on the south side of Richmond Avenue. Two years ago, few people patronized the nearly six-acre oasis on a dead-end street in Houston's Upper Kirby District. Now, Levy Park hosts thousands of visitors a week thanks to a nationally-recognized public/private partnership with Houston-based realty firm Midway.

In 2018, Levy Park — which underwent a $15 million revitalization and renovation — was named a winner of the Urban Land Institute's Open Space Award. The worldwide competition recognizes outstanding examples of successful large- and small-scale public spaces that have socially enriched and revitalized the economies of their surrounding communities and are selected by an international jury representing different facets of development.

Built with public funds and sustained primarily by private lease agreements with the Midway Cos., the park features activity and event lawns, a performance pavilion, dog park, promenade with seating, and games. Its community garden and rain garden both harvest and reuse stormwater. At the heart of Levy Park is the unique Children's Park, which offers imaginative, interactive sculptures, playful fountains and a one-hundred-and-fifty-foot-long tree house situated among several large legacy live oak trees that were relocated on site and provide a magnificent canopy.

Jonathan H. Brinsden, chief executive officer of Midway, believed the Upper Kirby area — with its critical mass of established neighborhoods and mature office development — needed more green spaces. "The area lacked a signature public gathering place to create the 'there' there," he continued. Midway signed a long-term ground lease for property that the company developed as a sixteen-story office and retail project, Kirby Grove, which has frontage on Richmond Avenue. Midway also developed a 270-unit, eight-story multifamily development, Avenue Grove, on the southern edge of the park.

"These two new properties generate a steady stream of people, restaurants and services, as well as revenue — populating a park is as important to its success as funding it. The buildings give the park an urban edge, buffering it from the busy streets to the north and south," Brinsden said.

Midway's ground lease provides a steady revenue stream that helps pay for park maintenance. The Levy Park Conservancy, an affiliate of the Upper Kirby Foundation, generates funds to support a full calendar of health, wellness, and cultural programming that is free to the public.

Houston is blessed to have some of the most innovative and results-oriented philanthropists anywhere in the world, adds Brinsden. "They take a strategic approach to investing in green space and trail improvements that transform neglected and underperforming areas," he explains.

"The public sector also is looking for partnerships as a way to accomplish more with their limited resources. That is why effective public and private partnerships make so much sense — together we can generate economic opportunity and benefit public health and safety with smart investments in green infrastructure, trails, parks, and open spaces."

— JONATHAN H. BRINSDEN, CEO OF MIDWAY

One example is real estate entrepreneur Robert Clay, president of Clay Development & Construction. Together with his wife, Emily, they have donated generously to the redevelopment of Memorial Park.

"Emily and I are lucky enough to have the ability to give back to the city that has given us so much," Clay explains. "It is a donation that we are both very proud of and hope to see others in the real estate community do the same. The vision of the new Memorial Park is a grand one. The overarching goal, though, is for Houstonians to be able to use and enjoy all fifteen-hundred acres of the Park, not just one hundred acres or so. The Memorial Park Conservancy has devised a master plan that allows this to happen. It's a $200-plus million project and they have raised all but thirty million dollars so far. Parks are important to all cities, but maybe in Houston they are even more important. Our city is huge, covering over 627 square miles — and most of that is concrete. We need as many green spaces as possible to allow every citizen to get out into nature and enjoy time with their family and each other."

A century ago, Houston real estate investor and industrialist George H. Hermann deeded 285 acres to the city for a municipal park across the street from the Rice Institute, and thus Hermann Park was born. A century later, Hermann Park is 445 acres of beautiful green space visited by an estimated six million people each year. Important to note: The park is rimmed with high-rise and mid-rise residential, medical office space, and the Texas Medical Center.

Parks have always been important in the city, but over the past several decades some have been neglected. Some one hundred years ago, Houston realized parks were important in the scheme of city development, emphasizes Stephen Fox, architectural historian and a lecturer at the Rice School of Architecture and the Gerald D. Hines College of Architecture at the University of Houston. In 1912, according to Fox, the newly organized Houston Park Commission engaged land planner Arthur Comey to prepare a Houston park plan, which was published in

1913. A year later, the Park Commission hired George Kessler — one of foremost city planners in the United States — to develop Comey's recommendations. Kessler laid out Hermann Park, the Shadyside neighborhood, Main Boulevard — now called Main Street, and other city parks. Then, the landscape architecture firm of Hare & Hare took over these jobs after Kessler's death in 1923.

> "Hare & Hare designed the parkways along Buffalo Bayou [Allen Parkway and Memorial Drive] and Brays Bayou [North and South MacGregor Ways]," said Fox. "Hare & Hare were the landscape architects of Memorial Park and the Houston Zoo. They did an enormous amount of work from the 1920s to the 1950s and left Houston with a substantial legacy of public space — most of it achieved between 1910-1940. Since the late twentieth century there has been renewed commitment to replenishing what proved to be a tremendous legacy for Houston — although the city is many times larger now."

One lasting legacy has been Buffalo Bayou. Flowing east some fifty-three miles from Katy through the Port of Houston and Houston Ship Channel into Galveston Bay and into the Gulf of Mexico, Buffalo Bayou has played an important part in Houston's history ever since the Allen brothers founded the city nearly two hundred years ago. Today, the 160-acre Buffalo Bayou Park is one of the country's great urban green spaces and received Urban Land Institute Houston's 2017 Development of Distinction Urban Open Space Award. Built through yet another public-private partnership, the $58 million undertaking was financed in part by a $30 million donation from the Kinder Foundation.

Anne Olson, president of Buffalo Bayou Partnership (BBP), helps steer the organization overseeing revitalization activities along Houston's Buffalo Bayou. The BBP board has raised an impressive $200 million for the waterway's redevelopment. Buffalo Bayou Partnership's transformative work will continue over the next few years, she said. BBP currently has several projects and initiatives that are underway for the future revitalization of Buffalo Bayou.

> "In downtown, we are making plans to extend the bayou trail from Allen's Landing to US 59 where it will join a trail currently under construction by TxDOT [Texas Department of Transportation] at the Houston Housing Authority's Clayton Homes facility," she continues. "We also have a major planning project underway along the bayou's East Sector. We have spent the past year gathering input from neighborhood residents and stakeholders as to what they would like to see along this stretch of the waterway."

Houston's bayous act as drainage and flood detention areas when they are needed. But when they aren't being used for that, they provide enormous recreational opportunities for the community. "When we built the park and developed our maintenance plan, we took into consideration the fact that we would have major storm events," says Olson. "Of course, we could have never anticipated that Houston would experience the heaviest rainfall in our country's history during Hurricane Harvey. In addition to having the necessary resources to maintain the park, we have a great park crew that has a system down when the flooding events occur."

Hurricane Harvey had a significant impact on Buffalo Bayou Park, Olson adds. "It really was a tale of two parks. The upper portion of the park looked almost the same a few days after Harvey and people were out and about walking and biking," she continues. "The lower section of the park, however, did not fare as well. Much of this can be attributed to the banks being under water for six weeks as the Army Corps released water from the reservoirs. Following Harvey, we hauled off over sixty million pounds of sediment, planted approximately four hundred trees, repaired footpaths and renovated the popular dog park."

Houston's flooding issues will continue, she added, but hopefully, the city will never have another Hurricane Harvey. "We have been working with a number of other environmental organizations on a project called Headwaters to Baywaters," she continues. "We recently received private funds to do research on the benefits of purchasing and restoring land along our bayous. These green spaces will help to absorb and hold water during storms. It is important that we have 'green infrastructure' as well as 'gray infrastructure.'"

The continued greening of downtown Houston has attracted new multifamily developments as well as new residents. One of the pioneers of downtown residential living has been Marvy A. Finger of Finger Companies. Finger was one of the first major multifamily developers to identify the potential of Discovery Green and built One Park Place, one of the most successful high-rise developments in downtown.

"We started working on One Park Place in 2005," recalls Finger.

"I had built The Museum Tower, a high-rise residential building in Montrose five years before and it was extremely successful. I was building apartments in a dozen cities in the US and every city had a viable downtown where a lot of people were living. But nothing new residentially had been built in downtown Houston for a while. Houstonians were not living downtown. People were living in the suburbs. Houston's population was over five million. There was nothing new in downtown Houston. I knew I could find three hundred forty people out of five million who will want to live downtown. I learned the city was thinking about creating a downtown park near the George R. Brown Convention Center. I got excited early on because the Kinder family was heavily involved, and I knew they would get it done in a timely and upscale manner. So, I focused on trying to find a tract of land in the area. I knew there would be pent-up demand for housing downtown. There was!"

— MARVY A. FINGER OF FINGER COMPANIES

Finger adds the more park area downtown, the better. "I'm convinced that it's one more good thing about our city — our increasing park land," he adds. "We work hard to get more green space. The City Parks Department and the groups like Kinder Foundation do a great job. Parks are a huge feature for people to migrate to the downtown area. I'd like to see the land where the Pierce Elevated is now becoming a park and then we will see midtown and downtown blend together."

Parks have assumed a bigger and bigger role in every city's quality of life; more people now understand that Houston must compete globally if it is to continue to thrive. "Here in Houston, we realized after years when little attention was paid to green space, that Houstonians want great parks and will use them," says Hagstette. "The challenge was identifying the funding for both up-front capital improvements and long-term maintenance, which to date has been addressed through generous philanthropy and creative solutions to maintenance and operations."

As city fathers and others work to extend great parks into more areas of the city, parks funding on a city-wide scale will be an important challenge.

> "Through initiatives like Bayou Greenways 2020, we are now spreading this change to neighborhoods throughout the city," Hagstette adds. "That project alone will create linear parks along all the city's major bayous and connect one hundred and fifty miles of hike-and-bike trails. There are also the SPARK park projects, which through philanthropic, city and school district funding, are adding twenty-five new parks in park-poor areas of the city."

The SPARK School Program helps public schools develop their playgrounds into community parks.

Midway's Brinsden notes that any place where people are living in denser, mixed-use developments, the parks have become the "living room" of their city. "There is also something very important about the public realm, where people from all walks of life, cultures, ages, and incomes can peacefully enjoy a beautiful public area together," he adds. "These places help break down barriers between people."

Houston's greatest parks opportunity for the future resides on the edges of downtown. The re-routing of the Pierce Elevated and Interstate 45 will open wide swaths of urban land for park development. Then, a new generation of real estate developers will seize the opportunity to build on a park's perimeter. Houstonians can then realize what they have not seen for years: Parks may be the city's greatest economic development tools.

10

A NEW LANDMARK: THE TEXAS MEDICAL CENTER'S DOUBLE HELIX

By the time you finish reading this paragraph, a surgery will have begun at the Texas Medical Center (TMC), a place where more heart surgeries are performed than anywhere else in the world — 13,600 annually — and a baby is delivered about every twenty minutes.

Houston's 2.1-square-mile medical district and neighborhood boasts fifty-four medicine-related institutions, with eight academic and research institutions, four medical schools, seven nursing schools, three public health organizations, two pharmacy schools, and a dental school. All of them are not-for-profit. Home to the largest children's hospital in the world (Texas Children's Hospital), as well as to the largest cancer hospital in the world (MD Anderson Cancer Center), the TMC offers over 9,200 total patient beds.

"The Texas Medical Center is the world's largest medical center with one of the highest densities of clinical facilities for patient care, basic science, and translational research," said Robert S. Parsley, co-chairman and principal, Colliers International. "TMC represents one of Houston's major economic drivers and core industries with an estimated regional annual economic impact of $35 billion."

Houston leaders created the TMC — the biggest of its kind in the universe — nearly a century ago. Hermann Hospital was the first hospital to open, admitting its first patient in 1925. Back then, the area surrounding Hermann Hospital was forest and swampland; today it is home to nearly five dozen hospitals, medical schools, and other institutions that host more than eight million patients each year, including 750,000 emergency patients.

"The growth of the TMC is the result of visionary thinking and great leadership," added Parsley. "Thanks to strong leaders at each of its member institutions, what started as a cooperative largely focused on infrastructure has transformed into an organization at the forefront of innovation and transformation."

The medical center has received tremendous philanthropic support of Houstonians and supporters from around the globe as the result of the care and treatment that many have received at the center's member institutions, Parsley said. "A recent example of the generosity of Houstonians is the $101 million gift from Laura and Rusty Walter to Houston Methodist Hospital to support neuroscience research efforts."

Houston's TMC is expected to grow even more prominent in the years ahead with the completion of its TMC[3] biomedical research hub. "TMC[3] will be transformational as an economic engine for Houston and the state of Texas," said Dan Bellow, president of JLL Houston. "It will attract life sciences companies and further the groundbreaking research that's already taking place. Just recently Houston scientist Dr. Jim Allison (chair of the Department of Immunology at MD Anderson) won the 2018 Nobel Prize in Medicine. That's the level of work that is happening within the TMC and this project will take all of that into the next generation. The life sciences industry will become a major economic engine for Houston in the future, and TMC^3 is vitality important to continued growth and diversification."

Boasting a thirty-acre translational research campus, TMC^3 will bring together scientists, clinicians and industry partners together in more than one million square feet of research space with the single focus of translating medical discoveries into commercial solutions. "TMC^3 establishes a dynamic hub in the center of the expanding TMC ecosystem, which has a campus of more than 1,300 acres and is one of the country's largest business districts," explained Abbey Roberson, vice president of planning at the Texas Medical Center.

> "The project will foster opportunities for collaboration. The design of TMC^3 will physically knit together multiple institutions, and its location will be a bridge connecting the northern part of campus, which focuses on clinical care, with the southern part of campus, where a great deal of research takes place."
>
> — ABBEY ROBERSON, VICE PRESIDENT, TEXAS MEDICAL CENTER

Beyond the research functions, the mix of uses on the TMC^3 property will support the development itself, the existing TMC campus, and the surrounding neighborhood, as well as the broader Houston community, said Roberson, who also serves as chair of the Houston District Council of the Urban Land Institute (ULI).

The centerpiece of the TMC^3 campus — resembling the indelible double helix shape of a DNA strand — will be a multi-story building spanning nearly the entire length of the complex. The shared facility will include core laboratories, restaurants, retail and commercial space. "TMC^3 will move Houston much farther into the forefront as a global hub for biomedical research, leading to more innovation in this great city that has repeatedly remade itself as a global leader for science and innovation," Mayor Sylvester Turner said. "More than ever, people who chart the course for the future will want to work, live and play in Houston."

The concept of the double-helix evolved out of the iterative design process — calculating a desired result by means of a repeated cycle of operations — during the initial master planning phase of the project, said Roberson.

> "The shape clearly has meaning for life sciences but also provides the campus with a unique central focal point that undulates — both horizontally and vertically — as it spans the entire length of the TMC^3 site," explained Roberson. "The building form creates spaces for collaboration as well as a variety of open spaces. We believe the helix — which visitors will be able to see from the sky as they fly into Houston — will become an iconic image associated not just with the Texas Medical Center but with Houston as a whole."

The double-helix development will be located north of Old Spanish Trail near William C. Harvin Boulevard. The TMC^3 will also help meet the need for more laboratory space. Around the Texas Medical Center there is a shortage of research and lab space, said Eric Johnson, national director of healthcare for the Transwestern real estate firm.

The stated goal of the TMC³ is to transform Houston into the "Third Coast" of life sciences competing with Boston and San Francisco in advancing research and discovery. "TMC³ will be transformational as an economic engine for Houston and the state of Texas," continued Parsley.

> "It will attract companies focused on life sciences, medical devices, and biosciences and further the groundbreaking research that's already taking place. The goal of TMC³ is to enforce and encourage collaboration among TMC institutions to break down barriers among the institutions and accelerate commercialization of new ideas and products that result from this increased research. This should make the TMC a more attractive place for investors. It is expected that a major focus will be on the development of new medical-device and biotech companies."
>
> — ROBERT S. PARSLEY, CO-CHAIRMAN AND PRINCIPAL, COLLIERS INTERNATIONAL

Groundbreaking is scheduled for 2019 with an estimated completion three years later. It is projected that the new TMC³ will generate a stimulus of more than $5.2 billion to Texas and create thirty thousand new jobs, according to a third-party economic impact study by Silverlode Consulting conducted in November 2017.

The base floor of the helix will contain plazas featuring restaurants, commercial, retail and entertainment space. TMC³ will also include a four-hundred-room hotel and conference center with fifty thousand square feet of space.

"The goal is to make this a place that's activated day and night," continued Roberson. "The top level will have a world-class park designed by James Corner, who also designed the famed High Line in New York City. Rising sixty feet above ground level, Helix Park will contain trails, gardens, green space, and more. Houston, like other cities across the country, is experiencing a parks renaissance. We know it's critically important to develop parks and green space if we want to continue attracting the world's top talent."

The TMC has been doing that for nearly a century. The Texas Medical Center was the vision of Dr. E.W. Bertner, who was able to prevail on the trustees of the newly organized M.D. Anderson Foundation to fund his vision of a medical center, said Stephen Fox, architectural historian.

"In the early 1940s, the foundation bought a quarter of Hermann Park, following a referendum in which fewer than a thousand people voted, to sell park property to the foundation," continued Fox. "It's interesting to go back and read accounts of the arguments the Anderson Foundation trustees made about the value of a medical center. They didn't articulate a philanthropic vision, but instead (and what now seems prophetic) described how healthcare could contribute significantly to diversifying Houston's economy so that the city was not totally dependent on oil."

Today, TMC member institutions are some of the largest, most cutting-edge organizations in the nation. Construction is booming. "The $3 billion under construction represents a significant investment in the physical infrastructure needed to advance human health and support critical research," said Roberson. "This growth is important to TMC, but more important, to humankind, as employees and researchers are curing diseases and easing suffering of their patients."

The TMC Innovation Institute is an example of the future development. Established within the TMC, the institute is shaping the future of healthcare by uniting promising innovators with the best minds in academia, science, and medicine. Its programs help startups streamline the development of therapeutic, diagnostic, medical device, and digital health breakthroughs in world's largest medical complex. "The TMCx Accelerator is an example of programs located in the TMC Innovation Institute," said Parsley.

> "The TMCx Accelerator program provides startup companies with shared workspace, a curriculum tailored to the needs of healthcare entrepreneurs and the guidance of over two hundred advisors from the frontlines of the industry. Companies have access to the world's largest medical center, all without membership fees or equity sharing. Another example of the growth of innovation development within the TMC Innovation Institute is the opening of a JLabs, a premier life science incubator empowering and enabling innovators to deliver life-enhancing health and wellness solutions to people around the globe."
>
> — ROBERT S. PARSLEY

TMC is a place that has no comparable precedent of its scale and composition elsewhere in the world, said Roberson. "Increasingly, we describe ourselves as a medical 'city.' Part of the reason we do that is because of our immense size and population — more than one hundred thousand people work here. But it also reflects the fact that we do a lot of things that cities do: provide amenities like parks, coordinate new and expanding transportation options, create spaces where people can come together, and develop infrastructure that keeps people and facilities safe."

TMC leaders have a strong commitment to invest in the key infrastructure of the campus — roads, utilities and flood protection systems are critical assets that allow member institutions to serve patients and research facilities twenty-four hours per day, seven days a week, 365 days a year.

> "Without significant investment in these assets over the years, we wouldn't be able to support the growing demand at TMC," Roberson added. "We saw the value of those investments pay off during Hurricane Harvey. We all remember when Tropical Storm Allison crippled the TMC in 2001. That didn't happen when Harvey hit Houston sixteen years later. Thanks to infrastructure upgrades and investments totaling more than fifty million dollars, the Texas Medical Center remained fully operational during the entire storm."

Much of the land at TMC is governed by a set of covenants that allow only nonprofit entities that support health, education, and research to use the lands controlled by covenants. While these restrictions allow the institutions to focus their investments on their programs and physical assets, they do limit certain for-profit organizations from the TMC campus, Roberson said.

Anything built within the boundaries of the TMC will be facilities owned and operated by a nonprofit institution, added Parsley. "For-profit institutions, such as commercial office buildings, hotels and retail centers are built around the periphery of the TMC," he continued. "For-profit hospitals like Hospital Corporation of America (HCA) also do not qualify for membership in the TMC."

In addition, land opportunities around the TMC are limited. Demand for land surrounding the TMC has continued to increase as both TMC and non-TMC medical institutions grow and expand, said Parsley. The boundaries of the TMC continue to grow as member institutions keep expanding their footprints in the market. Growth is mainly concentrated south of the TMC, where available land for expansion exists.

The TMC will continue to be one of Houston's economic growth engines. The tremendous scientific and medical discoveries will cause the TMC to grow as we watch the commercialization of discoveries made in TMC[3] and the TMC Innovation Institute, pointed out Parsley. Attracting the leaders in healthcare to the TMC will be another reason for its continued growth.

"With the leadership and investment of the TMC toward the goal of being the 'third coast' of medical innovation, they have established the baseline for a healthy, expanding, and profitable innovation ecosystem," said Parsley.

> "With attractive investment opportunities, we expect to see an increase in domestic and international life science venture capital firms establishing a permanent presence in Houston. In addition, Houston should aggressively recruit up-and-coming medical device and biotech companies to establish their headquarters in Houston. These represent both buyers of early stage innovation companies as well as supply-experienced management talent to feed the growing pipeline of companies. These two additions to the ecosystem will ensure Houston and TMC will succeed in having a world class ecosystem for commercializing medical innovation and generating a diversified source of economic prosperity for Houston."
>
> — ROBERT S. PARSLEY

The Texas Medical Center, which is just east of Rice University, creates major demand for housing and hotels in the area. One of the biggest projects is the new mixed-use development by Medistar Corp., a Houston firm led by Monzer Hourani. The massive development will include a thirty-three-story, 550,000-square-foot medical office tower at 6700 Main Street, a 353-room InterContinental Hotel and the thirty-five-story Latitude Med Center apartment tower featuring micro living units measuring as little as 339 square feet.

It is another example of the fulfilled vision of the founders of the Texas Medical Center long ago: Medicine is another leg of growth for the Houston economy and it will continue to generate new construction and new jobs for years to come.

11

THE GALLERIA: LET THERE BE LIGHT

IN THE BEGINNING, there was no Loop 610. Just farmland, a road, and not much else. Except a great expanse of high-potential property.

One other explosive element existed: the vision of local developer Gerald D. Hines, who wanted to build a shopping center in Houston — but not just any retail arcade. Hines carried inspiration from Milan, Italy, and a tour of that city's major domo of retail: The Galleria Vittorio Emanuele II — Italy's oldest active shopping mall and a major landmark in the country's second largest city.

Built in the nineteenth century in the center of Milan and topped by a glass dome, the four-story Galleria — named after Victor Emmanuel II, the first king of Italy — is majestic but also inviting. After a century of operations, it was still a focal point of life in Milan. Hines wanted his Galleria to be more than just a shopping center, too — the other downtown and epicenter of life in Houston, as was the original in Milan.

On November 16, 1970, Hines realized his vision with the opening of a glass-topped, mixed-use powerhouse of commerce. It was The Galleria, a fifty-two-acre development that now includes three million square feet with more than four hundred stores and restaurants, two Westin Hotels with a combined nine hundred rooms, and three office towers totaling one million square feet — and an Olympic-size ice skating rink — one of the first-ever built inside a mall. The rink below the Galleria's central glass atrium was included to increase foot traffic on the lower level, Hines later said.

Originally, when it first left the drawing board, the three-level Galleria was supposed to be four levels. But Hines' vision was scaled back to a more manageable three-story version. Now owned by Simon Property Group, the Houston Galleria is Texas' largest shopping center and the eighth largest nationally. It is also the most visited attraction in Space City, a place drawing more than thirty million visitors each year, including thousands of affluent international shoppers.

Hines' Galleria put the neighborhood on the map, kick-starting development in the area with its mix of location, access, and world-class amenities, said Sue Rogers, principal in the Houston office of Cresa, a large commercial real estate advisory firm. "And over the years its draw has remained as it's grown into a major business district rivaling many other cities' central business districts," Rogers continued. "The Galleria has always had the appeal of being a location that is centrally located as it sits almost midway between the popular Energy Corridor and the Central Business District. The Galleria is one of the few walkable submarkets where tenants can work, live, and play. Once the traffic enhancements are completed, the submarket should gain added mobility, improving access to the area's high-end amenities and making it even more desirable."

The Galleria did more than give birth to a business district. It energized Westheimer Road, also known as Farm to Market Road 1093, or FM 1093. The "Farm to Market" nomenclature is almost a comedic term given the urban, commercial nature of the multi-lane Westheimer thoroughfare today. For years after the opening of the Galleria, land investors considered Westheimer a golden spine for deals. Buying land along Westheimer and waiting for good things to happen was an investment thesis that resulted in handsome paydays for those with patience. In the early days, some real estate brokers called the area "Magic."

The Galleria itself was a home run for Hines. Nestled amid affluent neighborhoods — and not far from the blue-chip River Oaks enclave — the Galleria has become internationally known for its architecturally appealing, dynamic, mixed-use, urban environment. Department store chains earn their highest sales in the Houston area at the Galleria. Annual gross retail sales in Uptown District, which include the Galleria mall, exceeded $3.5 billion in 2016.

Real estate in the Uptown District boomed with mid-rise office buildings along the West Loop and an impressive skyscraper steps away from the Galleria designed by Pritzker-Prize-winning architect Philip Johnson and his then-partner John Burgee. Built at a time when energy companies were flush and sought impressive monuments to showcase their success (such as Pennzoil Place in downtown Houston), the 901-foot-tall landmark was known as Transco Tower until 1999 when it was rechristened Williams Tower. Many Houston natives still call it Transco, though.

Next to the Williams Tower is the three-acre Gerald D. Hines Waterwall Park, featuring a semi-circular architectural fountain that re-circulates more than eleven thousand gallons of water per minute as it cascades down the structure's walls. The fountain's designers crafted a "horseshoe of rushing water" opposite the Transco (now Williams) Tower. The semi-circular fountain is 64 feet tall, a foot for every story of the office tower. Surrounded by nearly two hundred live oak trees, the park is the community centerpiece for Uptown Houston and owned by the City of Houston.

Formally known as Uptown Houston, the Galleria area today is a mixture of office, retail, residential and hotel properties along Houston's West Loop from Richmond Avenue north to Buffalo Bayou and west to Yorktown. With more than thirty million square feet of commercial office space, Uptown Houston represents approximately fifteen percent of the city's total Class A office space — second only to downtown. Uptown Houston is the fourteenth largest business center in the US — more than twice the size of downtown Austin — and home to approximately two thousand small- to large-sized commercial businesses representing a variety of diverse industries.

Major employers today include:

- Canada-based energy company Enbridge Inc. (which acquired Houston's Spectra Energy, creating a $126 billion midstream giant)
- Landry's — one of the largest restaurant corporations in the United States
- BBVA Compass, a subsidiary of bank holding company BBVA Compass Bancshares Inc.
- And the headquarters of a large oil and gas exploration and production company called Apache Corporation.

The Galleria office market has not been impacted in this downturn (the 2015 to 2018 decline) as much as the west side of town and downtown, noted Dan F. Boyles Jr., a partner in NAI Partners office tenant representation group. "There was far less new construction during this cycle and most of it was tied to major tenants occupying all or a majority of the new space ," said Boyles, referring to BHP Billiton and Amegy Bank.

"However, it has had its challenges and there are still some that lie ahead. The pending relocation of Marathon Oil to the CityCentre area will put a large block of [Uptown office] space on the market in 2021. Additionally, we could see BHP dump more space on the market. Overall, I think the outlook for the Galleria area remains strong. The location, access and amenities are unmatched in Houston, maybe with the exception of Downtown. These things will continue to attract companies to the area."

— DAN F. BOYLES JR.

New development continues in the hotel sector as well. One example: Songy Highroads opened two hotels in the Galleria in 2016 — the 325-room Hyatt Regency Houston Galleria and the 157-room, select-service Hyatt Place Houston Galleria.

"We have been acquiring and developing projects in the Galleria since the mid 1990s," said David Songy, chief executive officer and co-founder of Atlanta-based Songy Highroads.

"The attractiveness of the Galleria market is that during the week, it is a strong business demand generator because of the thirty-five million square feet of office space in the area. Our weekend traffic is driven by the retail components of the Galleria. We have a significant base of business from Mexico that visits for shopping and weekend attractions. A third element is the Texas Medical Center. Although we are not in the TMC, a number of our customers choose to stay in Galleria area because of its amenities rather than the Medical Center."

— DAVID SONGY, CEO, SONGY HIGHROADS.

When it comes to development and building, Houston is a pro-growth, business-friendly environment; it is easier to get plans approved and start construction more rapidly in Houston than cities like Atlanta or Washington, D.C., said Songy, who recently refinanced the sixty-million-dollar construction loan on the Hyatt Regency Galleria.

> "Because Houston is so large, so diverse, and has so much to offer, hotels are faring better than other real estate sectors," Songy continued. "There is more concern for the office market, particularly in the Energy Corridor, than hotels. For investors, hotels are a safer bet. That's why we are in the Galleria with two new hotels."

Uptown/Galleria is one of the strongest office submarkets in the city primarily because of the live, work, play environment. Today, every office building along Post Oak Boulevard is within walking distance of restaurants or shopping. Residential growth has made the area even more popular and active at all times of the day, pointed out Dan Bellow, president of JLL Houston.

Uptown Houston offers more than six million square feet of gross leasable retail space — more than any other retail destination in Houston. The Galleria is home to high-end retailers such as Saks Fifth Avenue, Nordstrom, Neiman Marcus, and Apple. Uptown's thirty-four hotels have more than 7,800 rooms with the highest RevPAR (revenue per available room) in Houston.

Recent construction includes the nearby River Oaks District, a fourteen-acre outdoor mixed-use project inside Loop 610 with 252,000 square feet of retail, fine-dining restaurants, street-side cafes, and entertainment; 92,000 square feet of creative office space; and 279 residential units. The thirty-three story Arabella condominium tower opened just east of Loop 610 late in 2018.

Tilman Fertitta — the billionaire businessman and television star of Billion Dollar Buyer, who is the chairman, chief executive officer and sole owner of Landry's Inc. — recently completed a ten-acre mixed-use development called The Post Oak. Its thirty-eight-story tower by Fertitta, the owner of the National Basketball Association's Houston Rockets, is Houston's first vertical mixed-use hotel/office/multifamily/retail/restaurant development and includes the metro's first five-fixture (bathrooms with two sinks, toilet room, shower and separate tub) hotel.

The residential portion includes twenty-two rental units and the 140,000 square feet of office includes amenities like pickup service at the airport in a Bentley motorcar.

Uptown — less than six miles from Downtown Houston — is an urban environment with sleek high-rise residences and office towers along side high-end boutiques. Convenience is always a motivator for tenants in the Uptown market, added Rogers.

"The decision to be close to employees' homes or being centrally located with maximum amenities and freeway exposure is one that seems to change based on both employment growth and the potential to take advantage of competitive markets," Rogers continued. "Because the Galleria is continuing to add residential development and amenities where people can live, walk, or easily commute to work, and shop should help continue to make the Galleria a desirable place to be for tenants."

Each day, more than two hundred thousand people converge in Uptown Houston to work, stay in the area's hotels, shop in high-end stores or dine in cutting edge, chef-driven restaurants. One of the challenges in recent years, is that the Uptown Houston area — those dense, tightly packed six hundred acres in the heart of Houston — has become too popular. Choke-hold traffic blocks up Uptown regularly. Enter the Boulevard Project, designed as the $121.5 million savior from the threat of a crushing mobility problem.

"We are wrapping a mobility project into our efforts to create a much more inviting Post Oak Boulevard that is the very core of the Uptown Houston area," said John Breeding, president and chief executive officer of the Uptown Houston District. "Transit is the catalyst, but the key is the context of Post Oak Boulevard — pedestrian improvements are as important as anything else. We are developing a beautiful environment for Post Oak Boulevard."

In the last five years, Breeding notes, three billion dollars in projects have opened, including new office buildings — the first ones built since early 1980s. Also, some additional retail came online, and several hotels were built.

"The big growth is that we added 8,600 units of multi-family, some just being completed," Breeding continued. "The key is not only the densification of Uptown Houston but also the urban mixture that is happening. It's not only office but residential, retail, restaurants, and hotel. If it were all office, the mixture wouldn't be as appealing as it is now. Uptown Houston is a highly desirable place. It's a great destination for tourists as well as business travelers. There is high occupancy in Uptown Houston hotels even on the weekends."

Ultimately, Breeding continued, "we are not going to build enough freeways to get people where they want to go, so we've worked hard to bring transit to this area. We've worked closely with TxDOT, the Harris County Toll Road Authority, Metro, and others. We are engaged in a $200 million project that ties the area into Metro's Park & Ride system." Suburban dwellers will be able to drive from home to a Metro parking lot near their home, then ride buses to transit stations near Uptown. Then they will board high-capacity buses that transport them down the center of the Uptown District. "People will be able to live where they choose, whether it is Uptown Houston or the center city when this project completed. If you live in, say, Fairfield and need to go to Uptown Houston, you'll never have to get in your car to go to the West Loop. You can just take transit. It's an incredible addition for asset development."

The key feature of the Boulevard revamp will be the dedicated bus lanes that run down the middle of Post Oak Boulevard.

"In the first generation of operations, they'll be articulated buses, painted to look similar to the light rail cars. The buses will have three large doors — one front, one back, and one in the middle. The bus will pull up to one of eight elevated platforms along the Boulevard and the doors will open. If you are using a wheelchair, you can roll from the platform onto the bus, or you can take your bike onto the bus, similar to light rail. There will be eight well-designed stations over the two miles of Post Oak Boulevard, or the Boulevard as we call it."

— JOHN BREEDING, PRESIDENT, CEO OF UPTOWN HOUSTON DISTRICT

Pedestrians are not left out. "We will expand the four-foot sidewalks along the Boulevard to twelve-foot-wide pedestrian environments and more than double the amount of trees. In essence, Post Oak Boulevard has three hundred fifty live oaks," Breeding added. "When we finish, it will have over eight hundred and be a colonnade of green."

The real terminus for the bus system is wherever Metro's Park & Ride system is stopped. The system will take an individual to Katy or Sugar Land; a new Uptown Transit Center will be built to serve the Westpark Tollway and Southwest Freeway, allowing commuters and visitors to use the Park & Ride lots along these corridors. "The buses will come into and exit through the transit center and take the short jaunt to the Boulevard. We're building from I-10 to 59, and two miles of the four miles is on Post Oak Boulevard," said Breeding. "We're just connecting into the system."

To understand the impact of the Boulevard project, says Dan Bellow of JLL, Uptown's transit should be compared to downtown's. "Nearly forty percent of the downtown workforce utilizes Park & Ride to get to work," he said. "Uptown will be the first market outside of the CBD to be specially served by mass transit. When complete, those who work in the area will be able to utilize Park & Ride to get to work. Time will tell, but hopefully it will reduce traffic congestion, which has traditionally been a challenge for the submarket. I see the project as a positive."

Not everyone does. Boyles of NAI Partners notes it is already impacting the area and not in a positive way. "Traffic has gotten so bad because of all the construction; they are tearing up every street," Boyles said. "Realistically, I don't think it will have any impact, short of public relations to combat the bad image associated with all the congestion in the area. Will some people use the new buses? Yes. Will it have a significant impact? Not in my opinion. I read a statistic from the Greater Houston Partnership that said ten years ago 78.5 percent of all commuters in Houston drove alone. Today, it is 80.3 percent. People are driving their own cars and driving alone. Traffic is not yet like Los Angeles or New York City, but Houston has almost no mass transit infrastructure unless you are downtown. My hope is autonomous cars get here sooner rather than later."

It is also important to note that the Park & Ride bus system primarily serves commuters who live in far-out suburbs, not the thousands of shoppers headed to the Galleria. The traffic around the Galleria during Christmas shopping season may always be nightmarish. Several real estate professionals who work in the Galleria say they are taking a skeptical, wait-and-see stance before believing the new Boulevard transit system will make much of difference.

While the Marathon Oil departure will inflict certain pain on the submarket, one company relocating from Uptown is exceptionally noteworthy. It's the development firm that birthed the Galleria — Hines. The Hines organization will leave the Uptown/Galleria area — Hines' headquarters has been located in

Williams Tower for years — and move into more than one hundred thousand square feet in a tower Hines is constructing downtown on the former site of the Houston Chronicle building.

> "It's not a Downtown versus Galleria situation," said Boyles. "Hines decided to move to a newer building. Once Hines moves out, a block of space will be available in Williams Tower — which is fairly well occupied now. It's a block of space becoming available in a quality building, and it will likely get absorbed. I see it as an opportunistic move for Hines, to take advantage of all the benefits of being in a newer property. That's why corporate America is paying top dollar for new amenities such as food halls, more natural light, bigger floor plates, terraces and green space, etcetera."

But this is Hines making the move — a deeply experienced real estate firm that understands Houston and has made few mistakes over the years.

Only time will tell if other firms will follow Hines out of the Galleria — and if the Boulevard project will help alleviate traffic congestion in the area. Uptown has seen its ups and downs before when the Houston economy went through rough patches. Companies eventually re-filled Uptown buildings as office rental rates went down. However, the surge in high-rise and mid-rise multifamily construction changed Uptown in recent years and more density is coming. The Boulevard transit project will help transport people to the suburbs.

But Houston's Inner Loop transit network is incomplete and more connections to Uptown from Downtown, Midtown, and the Medical Center must be implemented in future years. The failure to bring Metro light rail connections to Uptown was a sin, and the city will pay a price for it someday.

For years, Houston's leadership has operated under the belief that autos — and freeways — can provide almost all of the city's transportation needs.

The Uptown-Galleria area will be the first Houston district to disprove the auto-centric principle as Houston's Inner Loop becomes more dense with high-rise residential. Uptown's Westheimer Road and Post Oak Boulevard will not suffice in the years ahead — they will become clogged arteries. More multifamily will be built. Single-story retail centers with acres of surface parking lots will be replaced by more dense development. Post Oak Boulevard still has several acres of grass-covered land destined to be the platforms for high-rise towers in the years to come. The new Boulevard mobility project will improve things for a while. But the day of reckoning is coming in the decades ahead. Unless the city's transit system advances significantly, the weakness in Houston's auto-centric transportation system will be exposed, someday, once and for all, in Uptown Houston. Other major activity centers have more traffic escape hatches, more transit infrastructure in place.

Uptown is the future battlefield where everything the city's leadership has believed about growth and transit will be tested.

12

PIERCE ELEVATED: TEAR DOWN THIS WALL

THE BOUNDARIES of Downtown Houston will be erased over the next decade.

The Pierce Elevated, a stretch of Interstate 45 that cuts across the southern part of downtown will be removed. Supported by heavy-duty structural columns, the roadway has been a barrier between Downtown and Midtown. The ground-level space under the freeway is a loud and filthy place, often used over the years by the homeless as a bed and a bathroom.

Its removal means a grotesque fixture of blight leaves the city for good.

The Pierce Elevated posed as a barrier, restricting the positive flow of development momentum between Downtown and Midtown. Secondly, the freeway relocation will blur the eastern boundaries of downtown. Where will Downtown end and EaDo (the redeveloping district just east of downtown) begin? Opportunities to realign the western edge of downtown are emerging also. A great sea change is coming.

Two decades from now, downtown Houston may be unrecognizable from today. By then, the central business district of Space City will boast a Green Loop — a five-mile pedestrian and bike circuit connecting downtown with adjoining neighborhoods, driverless cars, and no traffic lights or street signs — and an "Innovation District" housed in office towers built in the 1980s and 1990s that have been transformed into more collaborative space with more flexible gathering areas. At least, this is the vision of downtown planners.

Currently encircled by Interstates 10, 45, and 69, the Houston downtown of tomorrow will no longer have those concrete thoroughfares separating the central core from the surrounding lower-density communities. The Central Business District will mesh perfectly with the other areas that were left behind when the freeways were built.

And Houston's downtown of 2040 will have many more green oases including a grand public space similar to Klyde Warren Park in Dallas — a popular 5.2-acre park spanning over the Woodall Rodgers Freeway and connecting uptown with downtown Dallas — with traffic flowing underneath and people enjoying the outdoors above.

The downtown of Houston — the nation's fourth largest city — will undergo a transformation thanks to the North Houston Highway Improvement Project (NHHIP), which provides a unique opportunity to bring together parts of Houston that were separated when the highways were built decades ago. The Texas Department of Transportation (TxDOT), through the Project, has identified seven billion dollars in capital investments to support mobility and improve highway safety — and bring a more vibrant pedestrian life to downtown Houston.

"The North Houston Highway Improvement Project represents a once-in-a-century chance to literally remake our central city, not just along the Pierce Elevated but around downtown and in areas to the north," said architect Guy Hagstette, vice president, parks and civic projects, Kinder Foundation. Central Houston (a private, non-profit corporation), has worked for nearly a decade with TxDOT on managing the impact of the project and exploring opportunities with communities along the route. "The 'Green Loop' around downtown and a greenway along Little White Oak Bayou to Acres Homes being proposed by the Houston Parks Board are great examples."

Hagstette added it is clearly an opportunity to replicate Dallas' success with its internationally recognized Klyde Warren Park — only Houston's version will be six times the scale and a part of the even bigger Green Loop.

"With three sports venues and the George R. Brown Convention Center nearby, the park can be a neighborhood park for EaDo, a great introduction for visitors to Houston and its bayou trails system, and a sorely needed venue for the city-wide celebrations that are outgrowing Discovery Green and Eleanor Tinsley Park," Hagstette said.

Public and private city leaders are rethinking transit options based on the North Houston Highway Improvement Project, which calls for rebuilding the three highways encircling downtown and realigning Interstate 45 to the north and east.

"All the freeways around the country generally go through the downtown area and Houston is no different," said Ric Campo, the chief executive officer of Camden Property Trust and chairman of the Quality of Place Committee for the North Houston Highway Improvement Project.

"Here the freeways were built in the '50s and '60s. So today, when people think about downtown, they see it is a ring of freeways. You have I-45 on the west, the Pierce Elevated on the south side — which connects 45 to south 59 — and on the north side you have I-10. Because of the age of the freeways, a lot of bridges have to be fixed, but rather than fix them the way they are, TxDOT is going to make major changes in the freeways configuration."

— RIC CAMPO, CHAIRMAN OF THE QUALITY OF PLACE COMMITTEE FOR THE NORTH HOUSTON HIGHWAY IMPROVEMENT PROJECT

The relocation of these urban roadways will be monumental, like the changing of the course of mighty river along an international border. The boundaries of downtown Houston will never be the same. Prime urban real estate will be transformed. The road rerouting is similar to untangling a knot of twine.

"What's going to happen," Campo said, "is that 45 will be moved north adjacent to I-10 and side-by-side with 59 on the east side of downtown. 45 and 59 are going to be depressed and TxDOT will put a cap on it from George R. Brown Convention Center to the south and go all the way past the ballpark [Minute Maid Park stadium] to the north. There will be a green space park larger than Discovery Green put in place on the cap. That's a game changer. On the south side, the Pierce Elevated will be abandoned and could be turned into a high-line park or other green space."

The road work is not a dusty proposal sitting on a bureaucrat's shelf. It will definitely happen, government officials say.

"What's important is that the project is fully funded by

TxDOT and it should start in 2020 and be finished in 2026 or 2027," Campo said.

The road rebuilding will deliver strong economic benefits, officials say. HR&A Advisors, a consulting firm focused on real estate and economic development, analyzed the potential economic and community benefits of the plans for Houston. HR&A found that full implementation of the plan — ranging from highly activated regional parks to more intimate neighborhood gathering places and trails along the bayous to redeveloped green districts — would generate economic benefits of between $5.6 billion and $9 billion over twenty years. Implementation of the plan, HR&A says, will generate increases in the value of existing real estate assets, new real estate development, new visitor spending, and worker and resident attraction to central Houston.

Bob Eury, president of Central Houston Inc., said the Green Loop is the major recommendation of "Plan Downtown: Converging Culture, Lifestyle & Commerce." The report is the result of fifteen months' work with a very large, nineteen-member leadership group that was part of a 166-member steering committee. Central Houston conducted a huge public outreach, gathering input from a diverse group of interested parties.

> "It's fairly ambitious and is drawing the most attention," Eury added. "TxDot is moving forward with major reconstruction of the highways downtown. Infrastructure improvements are needed, and it can become opportunity to redevelop edges of downtown, to better connect downtown and adjacent neighborhoods."

The main lanes of Interstate 45 will be reconstructed to run parallel to Interstate 10 north and parallel Interstate 69 on the east side.

Then it turn and fall into the right of way of Interstate 45 toward Galveston. With this reconstruction, the Pierce Elevated would not be needed. "We still would have to have access to the west side of downtown; there would be smaller connector lanes to exits on the west side," said Eury.

"Once the realignment is completed, the Pierce Elevated could go away altogether or could be repurposed into a linear green space and reconnect downtown with midtown, the Fourth Ward, and Freedmen's Town, which were cut off in the early '60s when the freeways were constructed. On the west side by City Hall and Hobby Center, some of the buildings could be reoriented. There are some one hundred acres on the west side including the municipal courts, police, and fire, as well as the theater district. There is a tremendous amount of city-owned land in this area offering opportunities for new and redeveloped public and potentially private buildings."

— BOB EURY, PRESIDENT OF CENTRAL HOUSTON INC.

Building a park on top, similar to the successful Klyde Warren Park in Dallas, would be a welcome amenity for residents. "On the east side, the new freeway will be below grade — in a trench with a cap over the top — so there could be an open area like Klyde Warren Park in Dallas," Eury added. "The area in Houston contemplated would be considerably bigger with a larger amount of green space and it might be public space." The Klyde Warren park achieved something else — a significant increase in property values as land near the park became valuable locations for high-rise development. The Dallas park was a launch pad, and it is now ringed with new development, much of it high-rise.

Equally important are plans to "enlarge" central Houston. Although Downtown is still the largest business district in Houston, in recent years it has not grown that much in total employment, Eury continues, "so we've set a target of increasing employment by twenty percent. That may seem timid, but we must grow. We see it happening in two ways. First off there is a fabulous stock of buildings downtown built in the 1970s, 1980s, and 1990s. One of the things we're seeing in today's workplace is more collaborative space and more flexible gathering areas. So, there is existing product primed for transformation."

Additional growth will sprout as aging office properties are redeveloped, which will make them more attractive for corporate expansion. For example, Brookfield Properties recently spent $50 million for a redo of the Allen Center office complex. Brookfield Properties also purchased the 4.2 million-square-foot Houston Center complex in 2017 for $875 million and a major redevelopment is planned.

Another key to downtown's future growth is convincing more companies to move to there.

"The other piece obviously is new business. There are new state of the art office towers entering the market, including two developed by Hines and one by Skanska. Energy is important to us, but it is far more technological now than it used to be. With all that adaptability comes innovation," Eury said. "We're already seeing innovation and start-ups downtown and we're planning for a strong innovation district within downtown. The reason is simple: Research has shown that the number of patents correlates to the density of people, and downtown is the most dense area around."

Another benefit: the state-funded improvements mean Houston could have both faster-moving traffic and cleaner air — counterintuitive as that sounds. Motionless cars stuck in traffic produce more emissions than traffic passing smoothly. The improvements in design are expected to increase speed on Interstate 45 by twenty-five miles per hour, said Campo. "This would reduce the 'smokestack effect' that occurs when people are driving twenty-five mph slower," he said. "Going that extra twenty-five miles faster improves Houston air so much that some say Houston could be in compliance with the Clean Air Act just from this project."

Reconnecting Houston neighborhoods that were left behind by the highway construction is very important and so is the increase in parks and green space that will be a great addition to downtown. "It's one more reason for companies to be attracted to a downtown location," said downtown office broker Paula Bruns, vice president of Colvill Office Properties. "Downtown already has significant amenities — restaurants, hotels and apartments and it is very walkable. Removing the Pierce Elevated will make downtown more attractive for tenants, who have become more focused on workplace environments."

13

E-COMMERCE, PLASTICS AND THE UNSEEN ENGINE

HOUSTON IS BULKING UP. E-commerce and the need to store consumer goods in close proximity to the buyers created the need for distribution buildings in Houston. Huge warehouses are being built for Amazon and national retailers. Other warehouses have been constructed to serve Houston's massive manufacturing complexes of raw plastic, which is often shipped in bulk to Asia.

Growing demand launched Houston into a full-fledged construction boom in the industrial sector. About ten million square feet of new warehouse space was completed in 2018 and another ten million square feet was under construction — with even more space being planned. It was a near-record building boom for the industrial sector, according to the Avison Young real estate firm.

Houston's status as an international shipping leader is a key factor in the warehouse building boom. It is even more amazing, if the history is considered, that Houston became one of the nation's largest ports. That's because Houston's natural geography does not lend itself to being a deep-water port. Houston's gigantic wharves, its petrochemical complex, and the recent surge in warehouse construction are all predicated on a port that was willed into existence by Texas visionaries.

The beginnings of Port Houston: First there was the stream. Then came the dream. The stream was Buffalo Bayou, a waterway in what would eventually become the fourth largest city in America. The dream was making Houston a major center of commerce by creating an international deep-water port to transport crops and other goods throughout the world. The port plan was envisioned more than a century and a half ago and finally realized in the early twentieth century. Today, Port Houston is the largest port on the Gulf Coast and powerful economic generator that rumbles unseen under the hood like a V8 Hemi engine.

How did Houston, some fifty miles from the Gulf of Mexico, create one of the world's busiest maritime commercial facilities? It happened through the Houstonian formula of success: Have a dream, take a few risks, add a dash of political persuasion and mix it with some hard work and a little arm-twisting and — presto! Inland Houston became the home of a deep-water port. Houston's port is anchored by the Ship Channel, an industrial waterway more than a century old. The channel is home to some of the biggest companies in the world, making up the nation's largest petrochemical complex.

Stretching from the Gulf of Mexico to the city, the fifty-two-mile Houston Ship Channel is a *man-made* waterway for ocean-going vessels and a key pillar of diversity to wean the city's economy from its petroleum addiction.

The Houston Ship Channel, with the enormous complex of waterways and infrastructure, wasn't born. It was made. In the mid-1800s, the railroads were the primary mode of transportation. But Houston entrepreneurs longed for the city to have a deep-water port. Galveston with its Gulf of Mexico frontage was the major Texas port at the time. With its dominant position, Galveston shippers steadily raised their rates and displaced the customers who paid them.

In 1900, a powerful hurricane devastated Galveston — one of the worst natural disasters in American history, with a death toll in the thousands. Following the devastation in Galveston, Houstonians argued that a "protected" inland port in Houston would be superior to Galveston's exposed Gulf position. Within a year, oil was discovered at Spindletop, a gusher that would soon transform the region's economy. The agriculture sector was booming and Gulf Coast rice began to rival cotton exports, highlighting the potential for a deep-water ship channel into Houston.

Congressman Tom Ball (the town of Tomball was later named in his honor) came to the rescue. Ball proposed that Houston and the federal government share the cost of dredging the deep-water channel. The federal government approved the plan, and Houston became the first port created with federal money and local matching funds. Since the 1930s, many port creation projects have followed the "Houston model" with the requirement of local-match funding. Work on the deep channel started in 1912 and was completed two years later.

Today, Houston is an important gateway for cargo originating in or destined for the United States' West and Midwest regions. Port Houston ranks number one in the nation in foreign tonnage and has surged to be ranked fifth in container shipping, according to the Port and JOC Group's Piers data. In the first half of 2018, Trans-Pacific imports at Port Houston jumped twenty four percent, as improvements at the Port facilitated more imports through the expanded Panama Canal.

"Houston's Ship Channel is booming," said Mike Spears, managing principal, Lee & Associates – Houston office. "With oil and gas remaining inexpensive, the downstream industry is expanding, and downstream businesses are enlarging their facilities to export more product. We're now seeing the plastics industry exporting increasingly more product to China, where they produce items and ship them back to the states once complete."

Spears and others expect a dramatic increase in activity at

the Port in the coming years. Plans are already underway to make the Port bigger and better.

> "The Ship Channel has been dredged and can accommodate larger ships with the expansion of the Panama Canal," says Spears. "We expect it to be even greater, with the Port of Houston becoming an even bigger operation than it is today. There are also many permits out for new liquid natural gas (LNG) facilities, aside from the large amounts of LNG plants currently being built, so that LNG products can be shipped through the Port of Houston."

Although it is a mere six miles from Houston City Hall, the Ship Channel location is unknown to many Houstonians. The reason is simple. Residents can't really *see* the activities of the Port in contrast to citizens of, say, the Big Apple. They know where the Ports of New York/New Jersey are because the waterways are a vital part of the city's day-to-day bustle and commerce. New York/New Jersey's Ports were there first, and the city sprouted up around them. But Houston's Ship Channel is in the industrial district, hidden away, like an engine under the hood.

Not only that, but it flows *east* and most of Houston was developed to the *west* — the Central Business District and tony enclaves such as River Oaks, Tanglewood, and Memorial are all located miles to the west of Port Houston.

Although the Port is unseen by Houstonians who do not drive to the east side of the metropolitan area, the benefits of the Port churn throughout the regional economy. Port Houston's economic activity made Texas the nation's top exporting state for more than a decade, according to information provided by the Port. In 2017, Texas exports totaled more than $264 billion, up from nearly $229 billion in 2016, according to trade data from the US Department of Commerce.

The Port — and e-commerce — have spurred a surge in Houston's industrial real estate, a sector that has remained steady despite fluctuations in oil prices. A major increase in construction of chemical plants occurred in recent years, creating thousands of new jobs. The boom at the Port was an economic driver when Houston needed it most. The oil-price decline that began in 2014 punished the Houston economy.

But an era of low oil prices was a bonanza for the petrochemical industry, which uses oil as a feedstock for chemical production. Numerous refineries along the Houston Ship Channel surged. As the oil industry slowed, the petrochemical sector boomed. An estimated fifty-billion-dollars worth of chemical facilities were built or expanded in the region over the past several years.

"US exports of plastics are expected to rise exponentially in the next few years, and spending on chemical plants softened the blow from energy-sector job cuts," says H.T. "Trey" Odom, president and chief executive officer of Houston-based Avera Companies, a major player in the commercial real estate industry. Avera developed a number of business parks near the industrial plants concentrated in the Southeast Houston. "I believe Houston is poised for continued growth in this area, particularly with the addition of new LNG [liquid natural gas] terminals here and along the coast."

Houston will have continued steady growth, driven in part by the reasonable cost of doing business here.

Demand has increased for industrial parks outfitted with railroad tracks, said Mike Spears.

"It's created a demand for distribution space, and what they are making in the chemical sector needs to be distributed. We continue to export and import products through the Port of Houston and the more we do that, the more we need larger warehouse space. There is also a continued demand for rail-served space. The premium for a rail-served building used to be between 5 percent to 7 percent; however, today, with an increase in demand, that premium is upward of 15 percent."

— MIKE SPEARS, MANAGING PRINCIPAL,
LEE & ASSOCIATES, HOUSTON

Property for new projects is hard to find and land prices are strong. "At this time, there is a scarcity of land for development," Spears added.

The demand for low-rise office space has emerged on the east side an an underserved niche, although it is small compared to warehouse and business park construction, said Robert Clay, principal at Houston-based Clay Development & Construction. Clay even coined the term "Petrochemical Corridor" for the area that runs down Highway 225 from Loop 610 to Highway 146; the epicenter is at Highway 225 at the Beltway.

"Although I'm not sure it warrants a new term because we aren't certain of the depth of the market," Clay said. "The emerging office market is just that, emerging. We do not believe there will ever be a Transco Tower there, but there is certainly a need for low-rise suburban office."

Over nearly two decades, Clay has developed projects that range from a ten-thousand-square-foot office building to a nine-hundred-thousand-square-foot distribution facility. Since opening for business in 1998, Clay has developed more than two hundred and thirty industrial and office buildings comprising approximately 13.2 million square feet valued at seven hundred and fifty million dollars. Houston's industrial market easily absorbs the new development. "The area's vacancy rate continues to be very low, and demand high," he adds.

Houston has a combination of industrial industries that have mitigated a lot of the volatility found in traditional economic cycles, agreed Odom.

> "Petrochemical manufacturers, refineries, and the cracker plants that supply them, among other users, demand institutional and rail-served buildings that are in close proximity not only to the Port and its two terminals, but also each other," Odom adds. "That demand has grown significantly since we started looking for sites near the Port several years ago. We have been methodical about selecting sites that are developer friendly — located in jurisdictions that want to see positive development — and tenant friendly in their location and with respect to the burden of tax and other operational expenses are concerned. Many of the surrounding cities and counties near the Port have incentives that are attractive to these new and/or expanding tenants."

In 2018, for instance, Exxon Mobil began operations at its new 1.5 million ton-per-year ethane cracker at the company's integrated Baytown chemical and refining complex. The new cracker will provide ethylene feedstock to new performance polyethylene lines at the company's Mont Belvieu plastics plant, which began production in the fall of 2017. The Mont Belvieu plant is one of the largest polyethylene plants in the world, with manufacturing capacity of about 1.3 million tons per year.

"The abundance of domestically produced oil and natural gas has reduced energy costs and created new sources of feedstock for U.S. Gulf refining and chemical manufacturing while creating jobs and expanding economic activity in the area," stated John

Verity, president of Exxon Mobil Chemical Company, when the expansion was inaugurated.

Adding to Houston's rosy outlook is the Panama Canal expansion. The five-billion-dollar project to widen and deepen the Panama Canal — originally constructed in 1916 — is also expected to benefit the Port of Houston. After nearly a decade of construction, the long-awaited expansion of the canal opened in 2016, and it has made a difference in Houston.

> "Houston has started seeing a difference in demand in submarkets with Port access, and the expansion is certainly one of the drivers," Odom continues. "Port Houston is executing on $1.5 billion worth of projects to deepen the Ship Channel and expand and improve its facilities in the next few years in a direct response to the Canal's expansion. Those plans will allow for larger ships and higher volumes of traffic. Those improvements along with our proximity to midstream petroleum assets, industry, and the canal are likely to continue to continue driving growth and investment in the Port area."

As a result of the completion of the widening and deepening of its Bayport Channel, Port Houston is seeing rapid growth in the size of ships calling on its container facilities, according to former Port of Houston Authority Chairman Janiece Longoria. "We continue to highlight the need to widen the channel through the entire reach of Galveston Bay to handle increasing vessel sizes, and that the economic security of our nation is dependent upon safe, two-way traffic through the busiest waterway in the nation," she said.

Accordingly, warehouse construction is surging in Houston as strong job growth, recovering oil prices and the city's emergence as a major distribution hub has energized the industrial real estate sector. In the fourth quarter of 2018, sixty-three major industrial buildings were under construction and more new buildings were being planned, according to the Avison Young real estate firm.

With some exceptions, e-commerce suppliers drive activity in north and northwest Houston while the petrochemical industry creates demand near Port Houston.

Houston's industrial real estate industry is changing as retailers such as Amazon spearhead e-commerce. Amazon recently opened an 850,000-square-foot fulfillment center in Hines' Pinto Business Park in north Houston and a one million square-foot facility on Interstate 10 to the west, in addition to several smaller facilities. Big box retailers chimed in with massive new warehouses, such as Best Buy (550,000 square feet) and Conn's HomePlus (656,658 square feet).

> "It is a big positive for industrial because there is a need for more distribution centers, as well as a need for distribution space outside of the typical areas," says Spears. "The demands of consumers are pushing corporations to set up distribution centers within ten or twenty miles of every rooftop."

The e-commerce trend ushered in a new wrinkle in Houston's warehouse business — bigness. In the past, Houston distribution buildings were typically small — under 300,000 square feet to 400,000 square feet. In today's market, distribution buildings are often twice as big.

> "We're seeing more e-commerce and consumer products companies that are looking at larger distribution buildings in our market," said Walker Barnett, principal at Colliers International. "Historically, the large distribution centers have been Chicago, Dallas, Atlanta, and Los Angeles, but Houston's position is changing thanks to our continued growth and the port's ability to take more inbound containers."

Ryan Searle, an industrial broker at NAI Partners agreed: Houston has gained national prominence as a distribution hub. Building big warehouses for big-box retailers is a trend that will last for a while. Walmart, Home Depot and Ikea already have monster-size facilities near the Port.

Energy prices remain volatile — always a worry for the Texas economy. But as long as oil stays above fifty dollars a barrel, most energy companies can turn a profit and this injects growth into Houston's industrial real estate market.

> "With the energy business currently on a renewed growth track, the industrial market will continue to have a profound impact on the Houston economy," said Avison Young Principal Bob Berry, who noted that Houston began registering exceptional job growth in 2018 as oil prices rebounded.

To meet the demand for facilities, Houston real estate entrepreneurs think big and build large. Located adjacent to Baytown TGS Cedar Port Industrial Park is the largest master-planned, rail-and-barge-served industrial park in America — and the fifth largest industrial park in the world, according to Cushman & Wakefield. TGS Cedar Port spans fifteen thousand acres, with more than ten thousand acres still available for development. The master-planned rail-and-barge-served TGS Cedar Port Industrial Park attracts light or heavy industrial use, manufacturing of all types — waterfront operations and warehouse/distribution operations. The transactions at the development have been Texas-sized.

Case in point: As 2018 came to a close, Avera Cos. purchased acreage in Cedar Port and announced plans to build as much as 2,262,000 square feet of warehouse space (more than fifty acres under roof.)

Houston's industrial sector will have continued steady growth, driven in part by the reasonable cost of doing business in what's still called "The Energy Capital of the World," says Avera's Odom. "Bottom line to me — the amount of money put into existing and newly constructed chemical plants shows the investment these companies have made in Houston and shows they aren't going anywhere anytime soon."

ABOUT THE AUTHOR
Ralph Bivins

RALPH BIVINS

Ralph Bivins is editor of Realty News Report, an award-winning publication covering regional and national real estate news. Bivins covered real estate for the Houston Chronicle for sixteen years and earlier worked as a staffer at the San Antonio Express-News, the Lubbock Avalanche-Journal and the Clear Lake Daily Citizen. He was a frequent contributor to United Press International (UPI). Bivins, a former president of the National Association of Real Estate Editors, has won numerous awards from that association, including the Best Column award. He also won the first place Charles E. Green Award in business writing from the Headliners Foundation of Texas.

A veteran Texas journalist, Bivins has reported on storms, scams, politics, governmental mismanagement and the hotel-room murder of a West Texas priest.

Photo courtesy of John Everett

www.ingramcontent.com/pod-product-compliance
Lightning Source LLC
Chambersburg PA
CBHW070040230426
43661CB00034B/1441/J